DAILY INSTANT POT

COOKBOOK FOR BEGINNERS

1900 | Easy Yummy & Healthy Instant Pot Recipes for Busy Day, Explore the Endless Possibilities

Billy S. Smith

CONTENTS

Pork, Beef & Lamb

Poultry

Fish & Seafood 44

Desserts & Drinks 70

Appendix : Recipes Index 81

INTRODUCTION

Billy S. Smith, a renowned chef, food blogger and educator, has been at the forefront of the Instant Pot movement, using the appliance's multifaceted capabilities to create dishes that are both hearty and simple . This cookbook isn't just a collection of recipes; it's a collection of recipes. It's a testament to Smith's belief that good food should be enjoyed by everyone, regardless of time constraints or culinary skill level.

Drawing on his wealth of experience, Smith has curated an extensive menu of recipes, from comfort classics to international favorites, each imbued with his signature flair. But this cookbook is not only for the experienced, but also for the seasoned. It's a beginner's treasure trove of step-by-step guides, tips, and insights into what your Instant Pot can do.

The book begins with an illuminating introduction to the Instant Pot, a tool Smith says will be a game-changer in cooking. From pressure cooking to sautéing, steaming to slow cooking, he explains how these features can open the door to creativity and efficiency in the kitchen.

What sets Smith's cookbook apart is his passion for healthy, wholesome cooking. Each recipe is carefully crafted with an emphasis on fresh, high-quality ingredients. Whether you're looking for gluten-free options, a vegan treat, or a low-carb feast, this cookbook has something for every taste and dietary need.

More than a guide, Billy S. Smith's Instant Pot cookbook is a guide. It is a companion. Whether you're a novice exploring the wonders of pressure cooking for the first time, or a seasoned cook looking to expand your culinary skills, this book provides a path that's as rewarding as it is delicious.

Unravel the Magic Behind the Instant Pot

The Instant Pot, a name synonymous with efficiency and innovation in modern kitchens, has captured the hearts of culinary enthusiasts worldwide. This multi-functional electric pressure cooker is more than just a gadget; it's a culinary powerhouse that combines the capabilities of several kitchen appliances into one sleek device. At its core, the Instant Pot operates as a pressure cooker, harnessing the power of steam to cook food quickly and efficiently. The magic lies in its sealed environment, which allows pressure to build and dramatically reduces cooking time, particularly for foods that typically require long simmering or braising. It serves as a slow cooker, rice cooker, steamer, sauté pan, yogurt maker, and even a warmer. With the touch of a button, you can switch between these various functions, giving you unprecedented control and flexibility in your cooking.

How Does the Instant Pot Transform Your Cooking Experience?

Time Efficiency: By utilizing pressure cooking, the Instant Pot can dramatically reduce cooking time. Meals that usually take hours can be prepared in a fraction of the time, a boon for busy lifestyles.

Versatility: The Instant Pot functions as multiple appliances in one, including a pressure cooker, slow cooker, rice cooker, steamer, sauté pan, and more. This all-in-one capability makes it a versatile tool for various cooking methods.

Consistency: With pre-set programs and precise temperature control, the Instant Pot ensures consistent results. Whether it's a family favorite recipe or experimenting with something new, you can achieve reliable outcomes.

Energy Efficiency: Compared to traditional stovetop cooking, the Instant Pot uses less energy. Its contained cooking environment minimizes heat loss, making it an eco-friendly choice.

Nutrient Retention: Pressure cooking helps retain vitamins and minerals that might otherwise be lost during conventional cooking. This can lead to more nutritious meals.

Ease of Use: The Instant Pot is designed with both beginners and experts in mind. Simple controls, intuitive interfaces, and helpful pre-set programs make it accessible to cooks of all skill levels.

Space Saving: By combining several appliances into one, the Instant Pot saves valuable kitchen space. It's especially beneficial for those with smaller kitchens or limited storage.

Safety Features: With built-in safety mechanisms like pressure release valves and safety locks, the Instant Pot is designed to be user-friendly and safe to operate.

Healthy Cooking: The Instant Pot facilitates healthy cooking by allowing for oil-free methods like steaming and pressure cooking. It's a helpful tool for those mindful of their dietary choices.

Easy Cleanup: With the ability to cook entire meals in one pot, cleanup is simplified. Many parts are also dishwasher-safe, further easing the process.

Why choose an Instant Pot cookbook?

- **Tailored Recipes**

Instant Pot cookbooks provide recipes specifically designed for the appliance, ensuring that the cooking times, temperatures, and methods are optimized for the best results.

- **Educational Resource**

These cookbooks often include introductory sections explaining the features and functions of the Instant Pot, making them a valuable educational resource for both beginners and experienced users.

- **Diverse Culinary Options**

An Instant Pot cookbook often showcases a wide variety of cuisines and dishes, allowing you to explore new flavors and techniques without feeling overwhelmed.

- **Healthy Cooking Guidance**

Many Instant Pot cookbooks focus on healthy cooking, providing nutritional information and guidance on creating balanced, wholesome meals.

- **Building Confidence**

Following tried-and-tested recipes can build your confidence in using the Instant Pot. Gradually, you may find yourself experimenting and adapting recipes to suit your taste.

- **Efficient Meal Planning**

An Instant Pot cookbook can be an essential tool for meal planning. With a collection of recipes tailored to the appliance, planning weekly menus becomes more straightforward and efficient.

- **Support for Special Diets**

Some Instant Pot cookbooks cater to specific dietary needs such as gluten-free, vegan, or low-carb diets. This specialized focus can be a valuable resource for those with particular dietary preferences or requirements.

- **Community Connection**

Utilizing a cookbook that aligns with a broader community of Instant Pot enthusiasts can enhance your cooking experience, fostering a sense of connection and shared discovery.

- **Inspiration and Creativity**

An Instant Pot cookbook can serve as a source of inspiration, sparking creativity and encouraging you to try new dishes or put your twist on classics.

- **Gift Potential**

Paired with an Instant Pot, a cookbook makes a thoughtful and practical gift for friends or family interested in cooking.

In conclusion, an Instant Pot cookbook is not just a collection of recipes; it's a guide, mentor, and inspiration for making the most of this multifunctional appliance. Whether you're a novice wanting to learn the ropes or a seasoned cook looking to expand your repertoire, an Instant Pot cookbook can enhance your culinary experience, making it a wise and rewarding choice.

Who Stands to Gain the Most from the Wonders of an Instant Pot?

The Instant Pot, with its multifaceted features and user-friendly design, appeals to a wide variety of individuals and can be suitable for:

Busy Professionals and Families

With its time-saving capabilities, the Instant Pot is ideal for those with demanding schedules. It allows for quick and nutritious meals without extensive hands-on cooking time.

Beginner Cooks

Its user-friendly interface, pre-set programs, and multitude of available recipes make the Instant Pot an attractive option for those new to cooking, guiding them through the process.

Experienced Home Chefs

The versatility of the Instant Pot and its multiple cooking functions appeal to seasoned cooks looking to experiment and diversify their culinary repertoire.

Health-Conscious Individuals

Offering methods such as pressure cooking and steaming, the Instant Pot can facilitate healthier cooking by retaining nutrients and eliminating the need for excessive oils.

Small Households or Singles

Available in various sizes, the Instant Pot can be a suitable appliance for those cooking for one or two, minimizing waste and offering portion control.

People with Special Dietary Needs

The Instant Pot allows complete control over ingredients and cooking methods, catering to those with specific dietary preferences or restrictions like gluten-free, vegan, or low-carb.

Students in Dormitories

Its space-saving design and multifunctionality make it a practical choice for students with limited kitchen space, providing an all-in-one cooking solution.

Eco-Friendly Consumers

The energy efficiency of the Instant Pot aligns with environmentally conscious choices, appealing to those looking to reduce their energy consumption.

Adventurous Food Enthusiasts

For those who love to explore different cuisines, the Instant Pot offers the flexibility to try various global dishes, all in one device.

Elderly Individuals

The straightforward operation and safety features of the Instant Pot can be beneficial for older individuals who may prefer a more manageable and less physically demanding cooking process.

RV Travelers and Campers

The Instant Pot's ability to serve as multiple appliances in one can be a valuable asset for those traveling or camping, where space and convenience are paramount.

In summary, the Instant Pot's appeal is broad, catering to different lifestyles, culinary interests, and needs. Its design and functionalities make it a suitable appliance for nearly anyone, from cooking novices to culinary experts, busy families to solo dwellers. Its adaptability ensures that it can find a place in diverse kitchens, enhancing the cooking experience in manifold ways.

Measurement Conversions

BASIC KITCHEN CONVERSIONS & EQUIVALENTS

DRY MEASUREMENTS CONVERSION CHART

3 TEASPOONS = 1 TABLESPOON = 1/16 CUP

6 TEASPOONS = 2 TABLESPOONS = 1/8 CUP

12 TEASPOONS = 4 TABLESPOONS = 1/4 CUP

24 TEASPOONS = 8 TABLESPOONS = 1/2 CUP

36 TEASPOONS = 12 TABLESPOONS = 3/4 CUP

48 TEASPOONS = 16 TABLESPOONS = 1 CUP

METRIC TO US COOKING CONVERSIONS

OVEN TEMPERATURES

120 °C = 250 °F

160 °C = 320 °F

180° C = 350 °F

205 °C = 400 °F

220 °C = 425 °F

LIQUID MEASUREMENTS CONVERSION CHART

8 FLUID OUNCES = 1 CUP = 1/2 PINT = 1/4 QUART

16 FLUID OUNCES = 2 CUPS = 1 PINT = 1/2 QUART

32 FLUID OUNCES = 4 CUPS = 2 PINTS = 1 QUART

= 1/4 GALLON

128 FLUID OUNCES = 16 CUPS = 8 PINTS = 4 QUARTS = 1 GALLON

BAKING IN GRAMS

1 CUP FLOUR = 140 GRAMS

1 CUP SUGAR = 150 GRAMS

1 CUP POWDERED SUGAR = 160 GRAMS

1 CUP HEAVY CREAM = 235 GRAMS

VOLUME

1 MILLILITER = 1/5 TEASPOON

5 ML = 1 TEASPOON

15 ML = 1 TABLESPOON

240 ML = 1 CUP OR 8 FLUID OUNCES

1 LITER = 34 FL. OUNCES

WEIGHT

1 GRAM = .035 OUNCES

100 GRAMS = 3.5 OUNCES

500 GRAMS = 1.1 POUNDS

1 KILOGRAM = 35 OUNCES

US TO METRIC COOKING CONVERSIONS

1/5 TSP = 1 ML

1 TSP = 5 ML

1 TBSP = 15 ML

1 FL OUNCE = 30 ML

1 CUP = 237 ML

1 PINT (2 CUPS) = 473 ML

1 QUART (4 CUPS) = .95 LITER

1 GALLON (16 CUPS) = 3.8 LITERS

1 OZ = 28 GRAMS

1 POUND = 454 GRAMS

BUTTER

1 CUP BUTTER = 2 STICKS = 8 OUNCES = 230 GRAMS = 8 TABLESPOONS

WHAT DOES 1 CUP EQUAL

1 CUP = 8 FLUID OUNCES

1 CUP = 16 TABLESPOONS

1 CUP = 48 TEASPOONS

1 CUP = 1/2 PINT

1 CUP = 1/4 QUART

1 CUP = 1/16 GALLON

1 CUP = 240 ML

BAKING PAN CONVERSIONS

1 CUP ALL-PURPOSE FLOUR = 4.5 OZ

1 CUP ROLLED OATS = 3 OZ 1 LARGE EGG = 1.7 OZ

1 CUP BUTTER = 8 OZ 1 CUP MILK = 8 OZ

1 CUP HEAVY CREAM = 8.4 OZ

1 CUP GRANULATED SUGAR = 7.1 OZ

1 CUP PACKED BROWN SUGAR = 7.75 OZ

1 CUP VEGETABLE OIL = 7.7 OZ

1 CUP UNSIFTED POWDERED SUGAR = 4.4 OZ

BAKING PAN CONVERSIONS

9-INCH ROUND CAKE PAN = 12 CUPS

10-INCH TUBE PAN =16 CUPS

11-INCH BUNDT PAN = 12 CUPS

9-INCH SPRINGFORM PAN = 10 CUPS

9 X 5 INCH LOAF PAN = 8 CUPS

9-INCH SQUARE PAN = 8 CUPS

Breakfast

Savory Roast Beef Sandwiches

Servings: 8
Cooking Time: 1 Hour 30 Minutes
Ingredients:

- 2 ½ lb beef roast
- 2 tbsp olive oil
- 1 onion, chopped
- 4 garlic cloves, minced
- ½ cup dry red wine
- 2 cups beef broth stock
- 16 slices Fontina cheese
- 8 split hoagie rolls
- Salt and pepper to taste

Directions:

1. Season the beef with salt and pepper. Warm oil on Sauté and brown the beef for 2 to 3 minutes per side; reserve. Add onion and garlic to the pot and cook for 3 minutes until translucent. Set aside. Add red wine to deglaze. Mix in beef broth and take back the beef. Seal the lid and cook on High Pressure for 50 minutes. Release the pressure naturally for 10 minutes. Preheat a broiler.
2. Transfer the beef to a cutting board and slice. Roll the meat and top with onion. Each sandwich should be topped with 2 Fontina cheese slices. Place the sandwiches under the broiler for 2-3 minutes until the cheese melts.

Smoked Salmon & Egg Muffins

Servings: 2
Cooking Time: 15 Minutes
Ingredients:

- 4 beaten eggs
- 2 salmon slices, chopped
- 4 tbsp mozzarella, shredded
- 1 green onion, chopped

Directions:

1. Beat eggs, salmon, mozzarella cheese, and onion in a bowl. Share into ramekins. Pour 1 cup of water into your Instant Pot and fit in a trivet.
2. Place the tins on top of the trivet and seal the lid. Select Manual and cook for 8 minutes on High pressure. Once done, let sit for 2 minutes, then perform a quick pressure release and unlock the lid. Serve immediately.

Pecan Chocolate Chip Breakfast Oats

Servings:2
Cooking Time: 7 Minutes
Ingredients:

- 1 cup old-fashioned oats
- 1 cup water
- 1 cup whole milk
- ¼ teaspoon vanilla extract
- 2 tablespoons packed light brown sugar
- 2 tablespoons chopped pecans
- ⅛ teaspoon salt
- 2 tablespoons mini chocolate chips

Directions:

1. In the Instant Pot, add oats, water, milk, vanilla, brown sugar, pecans, and salt. Stir to combine. Lock lid.
2. Press the Manual or Pressure Cook button and adjust time to 7 minutes. When timer beeps, quick-release pressure until float valve drops. Unlock lid.
3. Stir oatmeal, then spoon into two bowls and garnish with chocolate chips. Serve warm.

Strawberry Cream-filled French Toast Casserole

Servings:4

Cooking Time: 20 Minutes

Ingredients:

- 8 ounces cream cheese, room temperature
- ¼ cup sugar
- 2 cups sliced strawberries
- 1 tablespoon orange zest
- 4 cups cubed bread, dried out overnight, divided
- 2 cups whole milk
- 3 large eggs
- 1 teaspoon vanilla extract
- ¼ cup pure maple syrup
- Pinch of ground nutmeg
- Pinch of sea salt
- 3 tablespoons butter, cut into 3 pats
- 1 cup water
- 4 teaspoons powdered sugar

Directions:

1. In a large bowl, cream together the cream cheese and sugar by mashing ingredients with the tines of a fork. Fold in strawberries and orange zest. Set aside.
2. Grease a 7-cup glass dish. Add 2 cups bread. Spoon in a layer of the strawberry mixture. Add remaining 2 cups bread. Set aside.
3. In a medium bowl, whisk together milk, eggs, vanilla, maple syrup, nutmeg, and salt. Pour over bread; place pats of butter on top.
4. Pour water into Instant Pot. Set trivet in Instant Pot. Place glass dish on top of trivet. Lock lid.
5. Press the Manual button and adjust time to 20 minutes. When the timer beeps, quick-release pressure until float valve drops and then unlock lid.
6. Remove glass bowl from the Instant Pot. Transfer to a rack until cooled. Sprinkle with powdered sugar.

Banana Nut Muffins

Servings:6

Cooking Time: 9 Minutes

Ingredients:

- 1 ¼ cups all-purpose baking flour
- 2 teaspoons baking powder
- ½ teaspoon baking soda
- ⅛ teaspoon salt
- ½ teaspoon vanilla extract
- 3 tablespoons unsalted butter, melted
- 2 large eggs
- ¼ cup granulated sugar
- 2 medium ripe bananas, peeled and mashed with a fork
- ¼ cup chopped walnuts
- 1 cup water

Directions:

1. Grease six silicone cupcake liners.
2. In a large bowl, combine flour, baking powder, baking soda, and salt.
3. In a medium bowl, combine vanilla, butter, eggs, sugar, and bananas.
4. Pour wet ingredients from medium bowl into large bowl with dry ingredients. Gently combine ingredients. Do not overmix. Fold in walnuts, then spoon mixture into prepared cupcake liners.
5. Add water to the Instant Pot and insert steam rack. Place cupcake liners on top. Lock lid.
6. Press the Manual or Pressure Cook button and adjust time to 9 minutes. When timer beeps, quick-release pressure until float valve drops. Unlock lid.
7. Remove muffins from pot and set aside to cool 30 minutes. Serve.

Georgia Peach French Toast Casserole

Servings:4

Cooking Time: 20 Minutes

Ingredients:

- 4 cups cubed French bread, dried out overnight
- 2 cups diced, peeled ripe peaches
- 1 cup whole milk
- 3 large eggs
- 1 teaspoon vanilla extract
- ¼ cup granulated sugar
- ⅛ teaspoon salt
- 3 tablespoons unsalted butter, cut into 3 pats
- 1 cup water

Directions:

1. Grease a 7-cup glass baking dish. Add bread to dish in an even layer. Add peaches in an even layer over bread. Set aside.
2. In a medium bowl, whisk together milk, eggs, vanilla, sugar, and salt. Pour over bread; place butter pats on top.
3. Add water to the Instant Pot and insert steam rack. Place glass baking dish on top of steam rack. Lock lid.
4. Press the Manual or Pressure Cook button and adjust time to 20 minutes. When timer beeps, quick-release pressure until float valve drops. Unlock lid.
5. Remove bowl and transfer to a cooling rack until set, about 20 minutes. Serve.

Walnut & Pumpkin Strudel

Servings: 8

Cooking Time: 55 Minutes

Ingredients:

- 2 cups pumpkin puree
- 1 tsp vanilla extract
- 2 cups Greek yogurt
- 2 eggs
- 2 tbsp brown sugar
- 2 tbsp butter, softened
- 2 puff pastry sheets
- 1 cup walnuts, chopped

Directions:

1. In a bowl, mix butter, yogurt, and vanilla until smooth. Unfold the pastry and cut each sheet into 4-inch x 7-inch pieces; brush with some beaten eggs. Place approximately 2 tbsp of pumpkin puree, sugar, and 2 tbsp of the yogurt mixture at the middle of each pastry, sprinkle with walnuts. Fold the sheets and brush with the remaining eggs.
2. Cut the surface with a sharp knife and gently place each strudel into an oiled baking dish. Pour 1 cup of water into the pot and insert the trivet. Place the pan on top. Seal the lid and cook for 25 minutes on High Pressure. Release the pressure naturally for about 10 minutes. Let it chill for 10 minutes. Serve.

Lazy Steel Cut Oats With Coconut

Servings: 2

Cooking Time: 25 Minutes

Ingredients:

- 1 tsp coconut oil
- 1 cup steel-cut oats
- ¾ cup coconut milk
- ¼ cup sugar
- ½ tsp vanilla extract
- 1 tbsp shredded coconut

Directions:

1. Warm coconut oil on Sauté in your Instant Pot. Add oats and cook as you stir until soft and toasted. Add in milk, sugar, vanilla, and 2 cups water and stir. Seal the lid and press Porridge. Cook for 12 minutes on High Pressure. Set steam vent to Venting to release the pressure quickly. Open the lid. Add oats as you stir to mix any extra liquid. Top with coconut and serve.

Peanut Butter And Banana Oatmeal

Servings:2
Cooking Time: 7 Minutes
Ingredients:
- 1 cup old-fashioned oats
- 1 ¼ cups water
- 1 large ripe banana, peeled and mashed
- 1 tablespoon packed light brown sugar
- ¼ teaspoon vanilla extract
- ¼ teaspoon ground cinnamon
- ⅛ teaspoon salt
- 2 tablespoons crunchy peanut butter

Directions:
1. In the Instant Pot, add oats, water, banana, brown sugar, vanilla, cinnamon, and salt. Stir to combine. Lock lid.
2. Press the Manual or Pressure Cook button and adjust time to 7 minutes. When timer beeps, let pressure release naturally until float valve drops. Unlock lid.
3. Stir in peanut butter, then spoon oatmeal into two bowls. Serve warm.

Breakfast Frittata

Servings: 4
Cooking Time: 25 Minutes
Ingredients:
- 8 beaten eggs
- 1 cup cherry tomatoes, halved
- 1 tbsp Dijon mustard
- 1 cup mushrooms, chopped
- Salt and pepper to taste
- 1 cup sharp cheddar, grated

Directions:
1. Combine the eggs, mushrooms, mustard, salt, pepper, and ½ cup of cheddar cheese in a bowl. Pour in a greased baking pan and top with the remaining cheddar cheese and cherry tomatoes. Add 1 cup of water to your Instant Pot and fit in a trivet. Place the baking pan on the trivet.
2. Seal the lid. Select Manual and cook for 15 minutes on High. When ready, perform a quick pressure release and unlock the lid. Slice into wedges before serving.

Strawberry Jam

Servings: 6
Cooking Time: 30 Minutes
Ingredients:
- 1 lb strawberries, chopped
- 1 cup sugar
- ½ lemon, juiced and zested
- 1 tbsp mint, chopped

Directions:
1. Add the strawberries, sugar, lemon juice, and zest to the Instant Pot. Seal the lid, select manual, and cook for 2 minutes on High.
2. Release pressure naturally for 10 minutes. Open the lid and stir in chopped mint. Select Sauté and continue cooking until the jam thickens, about 10 minutes. Let to cool before serving.

Ricotta & Potato Breakfast

Servings: 4
Cooking Time: 25 Minutes
Ingredients:
- 2 tbsp olive oil
- 1 lb potatoes, chopped
- 5 eggs, whisked
- 1 cup ricotta, crumbled
- ½ tsp dried oregano
- 1 tsp dried onion flakes
- Salt and pepper to taste

Directions:
1. Warm the olive oil in your Instant Pot on Sauté.
2. Place the potatoes and cook for 3-4 minutes. Add in eggs, ricotta cheese, oregano, dried onion flakes, ¼ cup of water, salt, and pepper.
3. Seal the lid, select Manual, and cook for 10 minutes on High pressure.
4. Once ready, perform a quick pressure release and unlock the lid. Serve immediately.

Light & Fruity Yogurt

Servings: 12
Cooking Time: 24hr
Ingredients:
- ¼ cup Greek yogurt containing active cultures
- 1 lb raspberries, mashed
- 1 cup sugar
- 3 tbsp gelatin
- 1 tbsp fresh orange juice
- 8 cups milk

Directions:
1. In a bowl, add sugar and raspberries and stir well to dissolve the sugar. Let sit for 30 minutes at room temperature. Add in orange juice and gelatin and mix well until dissolved. Remove the mixture and place in a sealable container, close, and allow to sit for 12 hrs to 24 hrs at room temperature before placing in the fridge. Refrigerate for a maximum of 2 weeks.
2. Into the cooker, add milk, and close the lid. The steam vent should be set to Venting then to Sealing. Select Yogurt until "Boil" is showed on display. When complete, there will be a display of "Yogurt" on the screen.
3. Open the lid and using a food thermometer, ensure the milk temperature is at least 185°F. Transfer the steel pot to a wire rack and allow to cool for 30 minutes until the milk has reached 110°F.
4. In a bowl, mix ½ cup warm milk and yogurt. Transfer the mixture into the remaining warm milk and stir without having to scrape the steel pot's bottom. Take the steel pot back to the base of the pot and seal the lid.
5. Select Yogurt and cook for 8 hrs. Allow the yogurt to chill in a refrigerator for 1-2 hrs. Transfer the chilled yogurt to a bowl and stir in fresh raspberry jam.

Vanilla Chai Latte Oatmeal

Servings: 4
Cooking Time: 35 Minutes
Ingredients:

- 3 ½ cups milk
- ½ cup raw peanuts
- 1 cup steel-cut oats
- ¼ cup agave syrup
- 1 ½ tsp ground ginger
- 1 ¼ tsp ground cinnamon
- ¼ tsp ground allspice
- ¼ tsp ground cardamom
- 1 tsp vanilla extract
- 2 tbsp chopped tea leaves
- ¼ tsp cloves

Directions:

1. With a blender, puree peanuts and milk to obtain a smooth consistency. Transfer into the cooker. To the peanuts mixture, add agave syrup, oats, ginger, allspice, cinnamon, cardamom, tea leaves, and cloves and mix well. Seal the lid and cook on High Pressure for 12 minutes. Let pressure release naturally for 10 minutes. Stir in vanilla and serve.

Banana & Vanilla Pancakes

Servings: 6
Cooking Time: 15 Minutes
Ingredients:

- 2 bananas, mashed
- 1 ¼ cups milk
- 2 eggs
- 1 ½ cups rolled oats
- 1 ½ tsp baking powder
- 1 tsp vanilla extract
- 2 tsp coconut oil
- 1 tbsp honey

Directions:

1. Combine the bananas, milk, eggs, oats, baking powder, vanilla, coconut oil, and honey in a blender and pulse until a completely smooth batter. Grease the inner pot with cooking spray. Spread 1 spoon batter at the bottom. Cook for 2 minutes on Sauté, flip the crepe, and cook for another minute. Repeat the process with the remaining batter. Serve immediately with your favorite topping.

Pumpkin Steel Cut Oats With Cinnamon

Servings: 4
Cooking Time: 25 Minutes
Ingredients:

- 1 tbsp butter
- 2 cups steel-cut oats
- ¼ tsp cinnamon
- 1 cup pumpkin puree
- 3 tbsp maple syrup
- 2 tsp pumpkin seeds, toasted

Directions:

1. Melt butter on Sauté. Add in cinnamon, oats, pumpkin puree, and 3 cups of water. Seal the lid, select Porridge and cook for 10 minutes on High Pressure to get a few bite oats or for 14 minutes to form soft oats. Do a quick release. Open the lid and stir in maple syrup. Top with pumpkin seeds and serve.

Maple French Toast Casserole

Servings:4
Cooking Time: 20 Minutes
Ingredients:

- 4 cups cubed French bread
- 1 cup whole milk
- 3 large eggs
- 1 tablespoon granulated sugar
- 1 teaspoon vanilla extract
- ¼ cup pure maple syrup
- ⅛ teaspoon salt
- 3 tablespoons unsalted butter, cut into 3 pats
- 1 cup water

Directions:

1. Grease a 7-cup glass baking dish. Add bread. Set aside.
2. In a medium bowl, whisk together milk, eggs, sugar, vanilla, maple syrup, and salt. Pour over bread; place butter pats on top.
3. Add water to the Instant Pot and insert steam rack. Place glass baking dish on top of steam rack. Lock lid.
4. Press the Manual or Pressure Cook button and adjust time to 20 minutes. When timer beeps, quick-release pressure until float valve drops. Unlock lid.
5. Remove bowl and transfer to a cooling rack until set, about 20 minutes. Serve.

Grandma's Country Gravy

Servings:6
Cooking Time: 16 Minutes
Ingredients:

- 2 tablespoons unsalted butter
- 1 pound ground pork sausage
- 1 small sweet onion, peeled and diced
- ¼ cup chicken broth
- ¼ cup all-purpose flour
- 1 ½ cups heavy cream
- ½ teaspoon salt
- 1 tablespoon ground black pepper

Directions:

1. Press the Sauté button on the Instant Pot. Add butter and heat until melted. Add sausage and onion and stir-fry 3–5 minutes until onions are translucent. The pork will still be a little pink in places. Add broth. Press the Cancel button. Lock lid.
2. Press the Manual or Pressure Cook button and adjust time to 1 minute. When timer beeps, quick-release pressure until float valve drops. Unlock lid. Whisk in flour, cream, salt, and pepper.
3. Press the Keep Warm button and let the gravy sit about 5–10 minutes to allow to thicken. Remove from heat. Serve warm.

Blueberry-oat Muffins

Servings:6
Cooking Time: 9 Minutes

Ingredients:

- 1 cup all-purpose baking flour
- ¼ cup old-fashioned oats
- 2 teaspoons baking powder
- ½ teaspoon baking soda
- ⅛ teaspoon salt
- ½ teaspoon vanilla extract
- 3 tablespoons unsalted butter, melted
- 2 large eggs
- 4 tablespoons granulated sugar
- ⅓ cup blueberries
- 1 cup water

Directions:

1. Grease six silicone cupcake liners.
2. In a large bowl, combine flour, oats, baking powder, baking soda, and salt.
3. In a medium bowl, combine vanilla, butter, eggs, and sugar.
4. Pour wet ingredients from medium bowl into the bowl with dry ingredients. Gently combine ingredients. Do not overmix. Fold in blueberries, then spoon mixture into prepared cupcake liners.
5. Add water to the Instant Pot and insert steam rack. Place cupcake liners on top. Lock lid.
6. Press the Manual or Pressure Cook button and adjust time to 9 minutes. When timer beeps, quick-release pressure until float valve drops. Unlock lid.
7. Remove muffins from pot and set aside to cool 30 minutes. Serve.

Crustless Power Quiche

Servings:2
Cooking Time: 9 Minutes

Ingredients:

- 6 large eggs
- ½ teaspoon salt
- ½ teaspoon ground black pepper
- 2 teaspoons olive oil
- ½ cup diced red onion
- 1 medium red bell pepper, seeded and diced
- ¼ pound ground pork sausage
- 1 ½ cups water
- 1 medium avocado, peeled, pitted, and diced

Directions:

1. In a medium bowl, whisk together eggs, salt, and black pepper. Set aside.
2. Press the Sauté button on the Instant Pot and heat oil. Stir-fry onion, bell pepper, and sausage 3–4 minutes until sausage starts to brown and onions are tender. Press the Cancel button.
3. Transfer sausage mixture to a greased 7-cup glass bowl. Pour whisked eggs over the mixture.
4. Add water to the Instant Pot and insert steam rack. Place bowl with egg mixture on steam rack. Lock lid.
5. Press the Manual or Pressure Cook button and adjust time to 5 minutes. When timer beeps, quick-release pressure until float valve drops. Unlock lid.
6. Remove bowl from pot. Let sit at room temperature 5–10 minutes to allow the eggs to set, then remove quiche from bowl, slice, and garnish with avocado. Serve warm.

California Frittata Bake

Servings: 4
Cooking Time: 10 Minutes
Ingredients:

- 4 large eggs
- 4 large egg whites
- ½ teaspoon sea salt
- ¼ teaspoon ground black pepper
- ¼ cup chopped fresh basil
- ½ cup chopped spinach
- 2 small Roma tomatoes, diced
- 1 medium avocado, pitted and diced
- ¼ cup grated Gruyère cheese
- 1 tablespoon avocado oil
- 1 pound ground chicken
- 1 small onion, peeled and diced
- 1 cup water

Directions:

1. In a medium bowl, whisk together eggs, egg whites, salt, and pepper. Add basil, spinach, tomatoes, avocado, and cheese. Set aside.
2. Press the Sauté button on Instant Pot. Heat the avocado oil and stir-fry chicken and onion for approximately 5 minutes or until chicken is no longer pink.
3. Transfer cooked mixture to a 7-cup greased glass dish and set aside to cool. Once cool pour whisked eggs over the chicken mixture and stir to combine.
4. Place trivet in Instant Pot. Pour in water. Place dish with egg mixture onto trivet. Lock lid.
5. Press the Manual button and adjust time to 5 minutes. When the timer beeps, let pressure release naturally until the float valve drops and then unlock the lid.
6. Remove dish from the Instant Pot and set aside for 5–10 minutes to allow the eggs to set. Slice and serve.

Lemony Pancake Bites With Blueberry Syrup

Servings: 4
Cooking Time: 24 Minutes
Ingredients:

- 1 packet Hungry Jack buttermilk pancake mix
- ⅔ cup whole milk
- Juice and zest of ½ medium lemon
- ⅛ teaspoon salt
- 1 cup water
- ½ cup blueberry syrup

Directions:

1. Grease a seven-hole silicone egg mold.
2. In a medium bowl, combine pancake mix, milk, lemon juice and zest, and salt. Fill egg mold with half of batter.
3. Add water to the Instant Pot and insert steam rack. Place filled egg mold on steam rack. Lock lid.
4. Press the Manual or Pressure Cook button and adjust time to 12 minutes. When timer beeps, quick-release pressure until float valve drops. Unlock lid.
5. Allow pancake bites to cool, about 3 minutes until cool enough to handle. Pop out of mold. Repeat with remaining batter.
6. Serve warm with syrup for dipping.

Appetizers, Soups & Sides

Chicken & Noodle Soup

Servings: 2
Cooking Time: 35 Minutes
Ingredients:

- 8 oz egg noodles
- 2 Carrots, sliced
- 1 tbsp Olive Oil
- 1 small onion, chopped
- 2 Celery Ribs, diced
- 1 Banana Pepper, minced
- 1 garlic clove, minced
- 1 small Bay Leaf
- 2 Chicken Breasts
- 3 cups Chicken Broth

Directions:

1. Warm olive oil in your Instant Pot on Sauté. Place the onion, celery, carrots, garlic, and banana pepper and cook for 4 minutes. Add in bay leaf, chicken, and broth. Seal the lid, select Manual, and cook for 15 minutes on High. When done, perform a quick pressure release. Transfer the chicken onto a cutting board and shred it. Put the chicken back in the pot with the egg noodles and cook for 7-8 minutes on Sauté. Serve.

Pea & Beef Stew

Servings: 6
Cooking Time: 35 Minutes
Ingredients:

- 1 cup mixed wild mushrooms
- 1 cup green peas
- 1 cup diced potatoes
- 1 lb cubed beef
- 3 sliced carrots
- 1 tsp red pepper flakes
- 2 sliced garlic cloves
- ½ cup dry red wine
- 2 tbsp butter
- 1 diced onion
- 2 cups beef broth
- 14 oz can diced tomatoes

Directions:

1. Melt the butter in your Instant Pot on Sauté. Place the onion and cook for 3 minutes until soft. Add in beef cubes and cook for 5-7 minutes until the meat browns. Add in garlic and cook for 1 minute until fragrant. Pour in red wine and scrape any brown bits from the bottom.

2. Put in potatoes, carrots, red pepper flakes, mushrooms, beef broth, diced tomatoes, and green peas. Seal the lid, select Manual, and cook for 15 minutes on High pressure. When done, perform a quick pressure release and unlock the lid. Serve immediately.

Old-fashioned Potato Soup

Servings:4
Cooking Time: 10 Minutes
Ingredients:

- 1 cup whole milk
- 1 tablespoon all-purpose flour
- 6 cups diced (½" cubes) Yukon Gold potatoes
- 3 tablespoons unsalted butter
- 4 cups chicken broth
- 1 teaspoon salt
- 1 teaspoon ground black pepper
- 1 medium yellow onion, peeled and diced
- 1 medium stalk celery, diced

Directions:

1. In a small bowl, create a slurry by whisking together milk and flour. Set aside in refrigerator.
2. Add remaining ingredients to the Instant Pot. Lock lid.
3. Press the Manual or Pressure Cook button and adjust time to 10 minutes. When timer beeps, let pressure release naturally for 10 minutes. Quick-release any additional pressure until float valve drops. Unlock lid.
4. Add slurry to pot. Use an immersion blender to blend soup in pot until desired consistency is reached, or use a stand blender to blend soup in batches.
5. Ladle soup into four bowls. Serve warm.

Carrot & Cabbage Soup

Servings: 4
Cooking Time: 25 Minutes
Ingredients:

- 1 cup canned white beans
- 14 oz can diced tomatoes
- 1 head cabbage, chopped
- 3 tbsp Apple cider vinegar
- 4 minced garlic cloves
- 4 cup chicken broth
- 1 chopped celery stalk
- 3 chopped carrots
- 1 tbsp lemon juice
- 1 chopped onion

Directions:

1. Place the chopped tomatoes, cabbage, apple cider vinegar, garlic, chicken broth, celery, carrots, lemon juice, and onion in your Instant Pot. Seal the lid, select Manual, and cook for 15 minutes on High pressure. When done, perform a quick pressure release and unlock the lid. Mix in white beans and cook for 2 minutes on Sauté. Serve.

Easy Chicken Broth

Servings:4
Cooking Time: 30 Minutes
Ingredients:

- 1 chicken carcass from a 4-pound whole chicken
- 2 large carrots, peeled and cut into chunks
- 1 small yellow onion, peeled and roughly chopped
- 2 bay leaves
- ½ teaspoon apple cider vinegar
- 1 teaspoon salt
- 6 cups water

Directions:

1. Place all ingredients in the Instant Pot. Lock lid.
2. Press the Manual or Pressure Cook button and adjust time to 30 minutes. When timer beeps, let pressure release naturally until float valve drops. Unlock lid.
3. Use a slotted spoon to retrieve and discard any large items from broth. Strain the remaining liquid through a fine sieve or cheesecloth. Refrigerate broth up to 4 days or freeze up to 6 months.

Homemade Chicken & Quinoa Soup

Servings: 6
Cooking Time: 25 Minutes
Ingredients:

- 2 tbsp canola oil
- 6 spring onions, chopped
- 2 garlic cloves, finely diced
- 1 carrot, chopped
- 2 celery stalks, chopped
- 2 chicken breasts, cubed
- 6 cups chicken broth
- 1 cup quinoa
- Salt and pepper to taste

Directions:

1. Heat canola oil on Sauté. Add in celery, spring onions, garlic, and carrot. Cook for 5 minutes. Add in chicken, quinoa, salt, chicken broth, and pepper. Seal the lid, select Soup/Broth, and cook for 15 minutes on High. Do a quick release. Serve.

Herby Whole Chicken Stew

Servings: 6
Cooking Time: 50 Minutes
Ingredients:

- 1 tsp cumin
- 1 tbsp butter
- 1 lemon, halved
- 1 whole chicken
- 1 ½ cups chicken broth
- 1 onion, quartered
- 1 ½ tsp Ranch seasoning
- ½ tsp lemon pepper
- 1 rosemary sprig
- 2 garlic cloves

Directions:

1. Combine the Ranch seasoning and lemon pepper in a bowl. Brush the chicken with the mixture. Melt butter in your Instant Pot on Sauté. Place the chicken and sear on all sides until golden brown. Set aside.
2. Fill the chicken with lemon, onion, garlic, cumin, and rosemary and place it in the pot with chicken broth. Seal the lid, select Poultry, and cook for 30 minutes on High pressure. When done, perform a quick pressure release. Let chill for 10 minutes before serving.

Curried Tofu With Vegetables

Servings: 4
Cooking Time: 20 Minutes
Ingredients:

- 2 tbsp sesame oil
- 3 green onions, sliced
- 3 garlic cloves, minced
- 1 celery stalk, chopped
- 1 cup mushrooms, sliced
- 1 red bell pepper, chopped
- ¼ tsp curry powder
- 28 oz firm tofu, cubed
- 1 cup bbq sauce
- 1 tbsp sesame seeds, toasted

Directions:

1. Warm the sesame oil in your Instant Pot on Sauté. Place the green onions, garlic celery, mushrooms, and bell pepper and cook for 3 minutes. Stir in salt and curry powder and cook for 2 more minutes.
2. Add in tofu, and bbq sauce, and ½ cup of water. Seal the lid, select Manual, and cook for 5 minutes on High. Once ready, perform a quick pressure release and unlock the lid. Serve warm topped with sesame seeds.

Mashed Sweet Potatoes And Carrots

Servings:6
Cooking Time: 9 Minutes
Ingredients:

- 2 tablespoons olive oil, divided
- 2 small sweet potatoes, peeled and diced
- 4 large carrots, peeled and cut into 2" pieces
- 2 cups vegetable broth
- 1 teaspoon garlic salt
- ¼ teaspoon ground nutmeg
- ¼ teaspoon ground ginger
- 2 tablespoons almond milk

Directions:

1. Press the Sauté button on the Instant Pot and heat 1 tablespoon oil. Toss sweet potatoes and carrots in oil 1 minute. Add broth. Press the Cancel button. Lock lid.
2. Press the Manual button and adjust time to 8 minutes. When timer beeps, quick-release pressure until float valve drops. Unlock lid.
3. Drain vegetables, reserving liquid.
4. Add 1 tablespoon reserved liquid plus remaining ingredients to vegetables in pot. Use an immersion blender to blend until desired smoothness is reached. If mixture is too thick, add more liquid 1 tablespoon at a time. Serve warm.

Beef Broth

Servings:6
Cooking Time: 30 Minutes
Ingredients:

- 3 pounds beef soup bones
- 2 large carrots, peeled and cut into chunks
- 2 stalks celery, cut into chunks
- 1 small onion, peeled and chopped
- 1 bay leaf
- 2 cloves garlic, peeled and halved
- ½ teaspoon apple cider vinegar
- 1 teaspoon sea salt
- 6 cups water

Directions:

1. Place all ingredients into the Instant Pot. Lock lid.
2. Press the Manual button and adjust time to 30 minutes. When timer beeps, let pressure release naturally until float valve drops and then unlock lid.
3. Use a slotted spoon to retrieve and discard any large items from the broth. Strain the remaining liquid through a fine sieve or cheesecloth. Refrigerate broth for up to 4 days or freeze for up to 6 months.

Vegetarian Soup With White Beans

Servings: 4

Cooking Time: 30 Minutes

Ingredients:

- 1 cup green peas
- 1 carrot, chopped
- 2 red bell peppers, chopped
- ½ cup white beans, soaked
- 1 tomato, roughly chopped
- 4 cups vegetable broth
- 1 onion, chopped
- 2 tbsp olive oil
- Salt and pepper to taste
- ¼ tsp dried oregano

Directions:

1. Heat the olive oil on Sauté and stir-fry onion, carrot, and bell peppers for 5 minutes until tender. Stir in green peas, white beans, tomato, broth, salt, pepper, and oregano. Seal the lid. Cook on High Pressure for 20 minutes. Do a quick release. Serve warm.

Warm Shrimp Dip

Servings:6

Cooking Time: 13 Minutes

Ingredients:

- Zest and juice of ¼ large lemon
- 8 ounces cream cheese, softened
- ¾ pound cooked peeled and deveined shrimp, diced
- 2 teaspoons hot sauce
- 2 medium green onions, thinly sliced (whites and greens separated)
- 1 teaspoon salt
- ¼ teaspoon ground black pepper
- 1 cup water
- ¼ cup grated Parmesan cheese

Directions:

1. In a medium bowl, combine lemon juice and zest, cream cheese, shrimp, hot sauce, onion whites, salt, and pepper. Transfer to a 7-cup glass bowl.
2. Preheat oven to broiler at 500°F.
3. Add water to the Instant Pot and insert steam rack. Place glass bowl on steam rack. Lock lid.
4. Press the Manual or Pressure Cook button and adjust time to 8 minutes. When timer beeps, quick-release pressure until float valve drops. Unlock lid. Sprinkle cheese on top.
5. Place dip under broiler 5 minutes to brown cheese. Garnish with onion greens. Serve warm.

Ukrainian-style Borscht

Servings: 4

Cooking Time: 40 Minutes

Ingredients:

- 2 tbsp grapeseed oil
- ½ lb beets, peeled, diced
- ½ lb potatoes, peeled, diced
- 1 parsnip, diced
- 1 celery stalk, diced
- 1 red onion, diced
- 2 garlic cloves, diced
- 3 cups grated red cabbage
- 4 cups vegetable stock
- ½ tsp ground cumin
- Salt and pepper to taste

Directions:

1. Heat the grapeseed oil in your Instant Pot on Saué and cook celery, red onion, garlic, parsnip, and red cabbage for 4-5 minutes, stirring periodically. Pour in the vegetable stock, potatoes, beets, cumin, salt, and pepper.Seal the lid. Select Manual and cook for 15 minutes on High pressure. When over, allow a natural release for 10 minutes and unlock the lid. Serve immediately.

Steamed Leek With Parmesan Topping

Servings: 2
Cooking Time: 10 Minutes
Ingredients:

- 3 leeks, cut into 2-inches long pieces
- 3 garlic cloves, crushed
- 1 tsp salt
- ¼ cup olive oil
- 3 tbsp lemon juice
- ½ cup Parmesan, grated

Directions:
1. Pour 1 cup of water into your Instant Pot and insert a trivet. In a baking pan, combine leeks, oil, garlic, and salt. Lower the pan onto the trivet. Cook on High Pressure for 3 minutes. Do a quick pressure release. Transfer to a plate and sprinkle with lemon juice and Parmesan cheese.

Cheesy Turkey Stew

Servings: 4
Cooking Time: 20 Minutes
Ingredients:

- 1 tbsp soy sauce
- 1 lb turkey breast
- 1 ½ cups chicken broth
- 1 cup sour cream
- ¼ cup grated Parmesan
- 1 tsp Dijon mustard
- ¼ tsp garlic powder
- Salt and pepper to taste

Directions:
1. Place the turkey breast and chicken broth in your Instant Pot. Seal the lid, select Manual, and cook for 10 minutes on High pressure. When done, perform a quick pressure release. Transfer the turkey onto a cutting board and cut it into cubes. Discard the broth and wipe the pot out.
2. Mix in soy sauce, sour cream, Parmesan cheese, Dijon mustard, garlic powder, salt, black pepper, and cubed chicken and cook for 2 minutes on Sauté. Serve.

Asian Tomato Soup

Servings: 8
Cooking Time: 20 Minutes
Ingredients:

- 2 tbsp coconut oil
- 1 onion, diced
- 1 tbsp garlic-ginger puree
- 3 lb tomatoes, quartered
- ½ tsp ground cumin
- 1 tsp red pepper flakes
- Pink salt to taste
- 3 ½ cups vegetable broth
- 1 cup coconut cream
- 2 tbsp cilantro, chopped

Directions:
1. Heat the coconut oil in your Instant Pot on Sauté. Place the onion and garlic-ginger paste and cook for 3 minutes. Stir in tomatoes and cumin and Sauté for 3 more minutes.
2. Pour in the broth and salt and seal the lid. Select Manual and cook for 6 minutes. When done, perform a quick pressure release. Mix in coconut cream. Puree the soup with a stick blender until smooth. Serve topped with red pepper flakes and cilantro.

Scrambled Eggs With Cranberries & Mint

Servings: 2
Cooking Time: 10 Minutes
Ingredients:

- 4 large eggs, beaten
- ¼ tsp cranberry extract
- 2 tbsp butter
- 1 tbsp skim milk
- 4-5 cranberries, to garnish
- 2 tbsp fresh mint, chopped

Directions:

1. In a bowl, whisk eggs, cranberry extract, and milk. Melt butter in your Instant Pot on Sauté. Pour the egg mixture and pull the eggs across the pot with a spatula.
2. Do not stir constantly. Cook for 2 minutes or until thickened and no visible liquid egg lumps. When done, press Cancel and transfer to a serving plate. Top with cranberries and garnish with fresh mint. Serve and enjoy!

Lucky Collard Greens

Servings:6
Cooking Time: 10 Minutes
Ingredients:

- 2 pounds collard greens, washed, spines removed, and chopped
- 1 small onion, peeled and diced
- 1 cup chicken broth
- ¼ cup apple cider vinegar
- 1 teaspoon sriracha
- 1 slice bacon
- ½ teaspoon sea salt
- ¼ teaspoon ground black pepper

Directions:

1. Place all ingredients in Instant Pot. Lock lid.
2. Press the Manual button and adjust time to 10 minutes. When the timer beeps, let pressure release naturally until float valve drops and then unlock lid. Discard bacon.
3. Using a slotted spoon, transfer collard greens to a dish and serve warm.

Baby Spinach With Beets & Cheese

Servings: 4
Cooking Time: 32 Minutes
Ingredients:

- 2 medium beets
- Salt and pepper to taste
- ¼ cup Goat cheese, crumbled
- 2 cups baby spinach
- 1 tbsp apple cider vinegar
- ¼ tsp brown sugar
- 2 tbsp extra-virgin olive oil
- 2 tbsp walnuts, chopped

Directions:

1. Pour 1 cup of water into your Instant Pot and fit in a steamer basket. Place in the beets and seal the lid. Select Manual and cook for 12 minutes on High pressure. When over, allow a natural release for 10 minutes, then perform a quick pressure release, and unlock the lid.
2. Remove the beets to a bowl and let cool. Peel and slice them into wedges. In a bowl, beat the apple cider vinegar, brown sugar, olive oil, salt, and pepper. Place the spinach, beets, and goat cheese in a serving bowl. Drizzle the dressing all over and toss lightly to coat. Sprinkle with walnuts and serve.

Curried Sweet Potato Stew

Servings: 4
Cooking Time: 15 Minutes
Ingredients:

- 1 cup almond milk
- 2 diced sweet potatoes
- 14 oz can diced tomatoes
- ½ diced bell pepper
- ½ diced zucchini
- 1 minced garlic clove
- 1 lime juice
- ½ tbsp minced ginger
- 1 diced onion
- 1 tbsp red curry paste
- ½ tsp turmeric
- 1 tsp curry powder
- 1 tbsp olive oil
- ½ tsp sea salt

Directions:

1. Warm olive oil in your Instant Pot on Sauté. Place the onion and cook until translucent. Add in garlic and ginger and cook for 1 minute. Pour in milk, sweet potatoes, tomatoes, bell pepper, zucchini, lime juice, curry paste, turmeric, curry powder, and salt, seal the lid, select Manual, and cook for 5 minutes on High pressure. When done, perform a quick pressure release and unlock the lid. Mix well before serving.

Bbq Pork Sliders

Servings:10
Cooking Time: 60 Minutes
Ingredients:

- 1 pork shoulder
- 2 teaspoons salt
- 2 teaspoons ground black pepper
- 2 tablespoons olive oil
- 1 cup barbecue sauce
- 20 slider buns

Directions:

1. Season pork shoulder with salt and pepper.
2. Press the Sauté button on the Instant Pot and heat oil. Sear pork shoulder on all sides, ensuring they are browned, a total of 8–10 minutes. Add enough water to almost cover meat. Press the Cancel button. Lock lid.
3. Press the Manual or Pressure Cook button and adjust time to 45 minutes. When timer beeps, let pressure release naturally for 10 minutes. Quick-release any additional pressure until float valve drops. Press the Cancel button. Unlock lid.
4. Transfer pork to a platter. Using two forks, shred meat. Discard all but 2 tablespoons cooking liquid. Add pork, 2 tablespoons cooking liquid, and barbecue sauce back into the Instant Pot. Press the Sauté button and stir-fry meat 4–5 minutes, creating some crispy edges.
5. Serve warm on buns.

Cheesy Jalapeño Sweet Potatoes

Servings: 4
Cooking Time: 35 Minutes
Ingredients:

- 1 lb sweet potatoes, sliced
- 2 tbsp olive oil
- Salt to taste
- 1 jalapeño pepper, sliced

Directions:

1. Pour 1 cup of water into your Instant Pot and fit in a steamer basket. Place in the sweet potatoes and seal the lid. Select Manual and cook for 15 minutes on High.
2. Once ready, perform a quick pressure release and unlock the lid. Warm the olive oil in the pot on Sauté. Add in sweet potatoes and Sauté for 3-5 minutes. Sprinkle salt and pepper. Serve scattered with jalapeño slices.

Pork, Beef & Lamb

Pork With Onions & Cream Sauce

Servings: 6
Cooking Time: 52 Minutes
Ingredients:

- 1 ½ lb pork shoulder, cut into pieces
- 2 onions, chopped
- 1 ½ cups sour cream
- 1 cup tomato puree
- ½ tbsp cilantro
- ¼ tsp cumin
- ¼ tsp cayenne pepper
- 1 garlic clove, minced
- Salt and pepper to taste

Directions:

1. Coat with cooking spray the inner pot and add the pork. Cook for 3-4 minutes on Sauté until lightly browned. Add onions and garlic and cook for 3 minutes until fragrant. Press Cancel. Stir in sour cream, tomato puree, cilantro, cumin, cayenne pepper, salt, and pepper and seal the lid. Select Soup/Broth and cook for 30 minutes on High. Let sit for 5 minutes before quickly release the pressure.

Pork Chops With Creamy Gravy & Broccoli

Servings: 6
Cooking Time: 35 Minutes
Ingredients:

- Pork Chops
- Salt and pepper to taste
- 1 tsp garlic powder
- 1 tsp onion powder
- 1 tsp red pepper flakes
- 6 boneless pork chops
- 10 broccoli florets
- 1 cup vegetable stock
- ¼ cup butter, melted
- ¼ cup milk
- Gravy
- 3 tbsp flour
- ½ cup heavy cream
- Salt and pepper to taste

Directions:

1. Combine salt, garlic powder, pepper flakes, onion, and pepper. Rub the mixture onto pork chops. Place stock, milk, and broccoli in the Instant Pot. Lay the pork chops on top. Seal the lid and cook for 15 minutes on High Pressure. Release the pressure quickly.
2. Transfer the pork chops and broccoli to a plate. Press Sauté and simmer the liquid remaining in the pot. Mix cream and flour. Pour into the simmering liquid and cook for 4 to 6 minutes until thickened and bubbly. Season with pepper and salt. Top the chops with gravy, drizzle butter over broccoli, and serve.

Honey & White Wine Pork

Servings: 4
Cooking Time: 40 Minutes
Ingredients:

- 1 lb pork loin, cut into chunks
- 15 oz canned peaches, chopped
- 2 tbsp white wine
- ¼ cup beef stock
- 2 tbsp sweet chili sauce
- 2 tbsp honey
- 2 tbsp soy sauce
- 2 tbsp cornstarch

Directions:

1. Into the pot, mix soy sauce, beef stock, wine, honey, the juice from the canned peaches, and sweet chili sauce. Stir in pork to coat. Seal the lid and cook on High Pressure for 5 minutes. Release pressure naturally for 10 minutes. Unlock the lid. Remove the pork to a serving plate.

2. In a bowl, mix ¼ cup water with cornstarch until well dissolved and stir it in the pot. Press Sauté. Cook for 5 minutes until you obtain the desired thick consistency. Add in the peaches and stir well for 2 minutes. Serve the pork topped with the peach sauce. Enjoy!

Easy Wax Beans With Ground Beef

Servings: 4
Cooking Time: 20 Minutes
Ingredients:

- 1 lb ground beef
- 1 lb wax beans
- 1 small onion, chopped
- 1 tbsp tomato paste
- 2 cups beef broth
- 2 garlic cloves, crushed
- 2 tbsp olive oil
- 2 tbsp parsley, chopped
- 1 tsp salt
- ½ tsp paprika
- 1 tbsp Parmesan, grated

Directions:

1. Grease the pot with olive oil. Stir-fry the onion and garlic for a few minutes until translucent on Sauté. Add beef, tomato paste, parsley, salt, and paprika. Cook for 5 more minutes, stirring constantly. Add wax beans and beef broth. Press Cancel and seal the lid. Cook on High Pressure for 4 minutes. Do a natural release. Carefully unlock the lid. Top with Parmesan and serve hot.

Mediterranean Lamb

Servings: 4
Cooking Time: 55 Minutes
Ingredients:
- 1 lb lamb meat, cut into strips
- 1 tsp vegetable oil
- 4 tomatoes, chopped
- 2 tbsp tomato paste
- 1 red bell pepper, sliced
- 2 garlic cloves, minced
- 1 yellow onion, chopped
- 1 carrot, sliced
- 2 thyme sprigs
- ½ cup dry white wine
- 10 black olives, sliced
- Salt and pepper to taste
- 2 tbsp parsley, chopped

Directions:
1. Warm oil in your Instant Pot on Sauté. Add in lamb and cook for 8 minutes on all sides. Stir in tomatoes, tomato paste, bell pepper, garlic, onion, carrots, salt, pepper and sauté for 5 more minutes. Pour in wine and enough water to cover everything. Add in thyme sprigs and olives. Seal the lid, select Manual, and cook for 30 minutes on High.
2. Once done, perform a quick pressure release and unlock the lid. Remove the lamb to a plate, discard bones and shred it. Put the shredded lamb back to the pot and stir parsley. Serve immediately.

Leg Of Lamb With Garlic And Pancetta

Servings: 6
Cooking Time: 40 Minutes
Ingredients:
- 2 lb lamb leg
- 6 garlic cloves
- 1 large onion, chopped
- 6 pancetta slices
- 1 tsp rosemary
- Salt and pepper to taste
- 2 tbsp oil
- 3 cups beef broth

Directions:
1. Heat the oil in your Instant Pot on Sauté. Add the pancetta and onion, making two layers. Season with salt and pepper and cook for 3 minutes until lightly browned.
2. Place the lamb on a separate dish. Using a sharp knife, make 6 incisions into the meat and place a garlic clove in each. Rub the meat with rosemary and transfer to the pot. Press Cancel and pour in the beef broth. Seal the lid and cook on High Pressure for 25 minutes. When done, do a natural pressure release. Serve.

Asian Pork & Noodle Soup

Servings: 4
Cooking Time: 60 Minutes
Ingredients:

- 1 lb pork tenderloin, cut into strips
- 1 piece fresh ginger, halved lengthwise
- 2 tbsp olive oil
- 1 yellow onion, halved
- 2 tsp fennel seeds
- 1 tsp red pepper flakes
- ½ tsp coriander seeds
- 2-star anise
- Salt and pepper to taste
- 8 oz rice noodles
- 1 lime, cut into wedges
- 2 tbsp cilantro, chopped

Directions:

1. Warm oil on Sauté. Cook ginger and onion for 4 minutes. Add in flakes, fennel seeds, anise, and coriander seeds and cook for 1 minute as you stir. Add in 4 cups of water, salt, pepper, and pork. Seal the lid and cook on High Pressure for 30 minutes.
2. Soak the rice noodles in hot water for 8 minutes until softened and pliable. Stop the cooking process by draining and rinsing with cold water. Separate the noodles into 4 soup bowls.
3. Release the pressure naturally for 10 minutes. Remove the pork from the cooker and ladle among the bowls. Strain the broth to get rid of solids. Pour it over the pork and noodles. Season with red pepper flakes. Garnish with lime wedges and cilantro leaves and serve.

Pork Loin With Pineapple Sauce

Servings: 6
Cooking Time: 35 Minutes
Ingredients:

- 2 lb pork loin, cut into 6 equal pieces
- 16 oz canned pineapples
- 1 cup vegetable broth
- 1 tbsp brown sugar
- 3 tbsp olive oil
- ½ cup tomato paste
- 1 cup sliced onions
- ½ tsp ginger, grated
- Salt and pepper to taste
- ¼ cup tamari
- ¼ cup rice wine vinegar
- ½ tbsp cornstarch

Directions:

1. Heat the 2 tbsp oil on Sauté. Cook the onions for 3 minutes until translucent. Add the pork and stir in pineapples, sugar, broth, tomato paste, ginger, salt, pepper, tamari, and rice vinegar. Seal the lid and cook for 20 minutes on Soup/Broth on High. Release the pressure quickly. Mix cornstarch and 1 tbsp water and stir it in the pot. Cook for 2 minutes or until thickened on Sauté. Serve hot.

Spiced Pork With Garbanzo Beans

Servings: 4
Cooking Time: 60 Minutes
Ingredients:

- 1 ½ tbsp vegetable oil
- 1 ½ lb pork shoulder, diced
- 1 red onion, sliced
- 1 cup garbanzo beans, soaked
- 3 cups chicken broth
- 1 cup tomatoes, chopped
- 2 garlic cloves, minced
- 2 tbsp fresh dill, chopped
- ½ tsp ground mustard
- ½ tsp paprika
- ½ tsp dried thyme
- ½ tsp cayenne pepper
- ½ tsp garlic powder
- Salt and pepper to taste

Directions:

1. Mix the paprika, thyme, cayenne pepper, garlic powder, salt, and pepper in a bowl. Sprinkle pork with this mixture. Warm the vegetable oil in your Instant Pot on Sauté. Place in pork and brown for 4-5 minutes.

2. Remove to a bowl. Add red onion and garlic to the pot and cook for 2 minutes. Pour in chicken broth and scrape any brown bits from the bottom. Add in garbanzo beans, tomatoes, and mustard and seal the lid. Select Manual and cook for 30 minutes on High pressure. When over, allow a natural release for 10 minutes and unlock the lid. Garnish with dill and serve.

Pancetta Kale With Chickpeas

Servings: 4
Cooking Time: 35 Minutes
Ingredients:

- 2 oz onion soup mix
- ¼ cup olive oil
- 1 tbsp garlic, minced
- 1 cup canned chickpeas
- 2 tsp mustard
- ½ lb pancetta slices, chopped
- 1 onion, chopped
- 1 cup kale, chopped
- Salt and pepper to taste

Directions:

1. Heat the oil and cook the onion, garlic, and pancetta for 5 minutes on Sauté. Add 1 cup of water, soup mix, salt, and pepper, and cook for 5 more minutes. Then, add the chickpeas and 2 cups of water. Add in the kale and mustard. Seal the lid and cook for 15 minutes on Pressure Cook on High Pressure. Once done, perform a quick pressure release. Serve immediately.

Beef & Jasmine Rice Porridge

Servings: 6
Cooking Time: 50 Minutes
Ingredients:

- 1 cup jasmine rice
- 2 cloves garlic, minced
- 1-inch piece ginger, minced
- 6 cups beef stock
- 1 cup kale, chopped
- 1 cup water
- 2 lb ground beef
- Salt and pepper to taste
- Fresh cilantro, chopped

Directions:

1. Run cold water and rinse rice. Add garlic, rice, and ginger into the pot. Pour water and stock into the pot and Spread the beef on top of rice. Seal the lid and cook on High Pressure for 30 minutes. Release pressure naturally for 10 minutes. Stir in kale to obtain the desired consistency. Season with pepper and salt. Top with cilantro to serve.

Garlic Lamb With Thyme

Servings: 4
Cooking Time: 60 Minutes
Ingredients:

- 2 lb lamb, cubed
- 2 garlic cloves, minced
- 1 cup onions, chopped
- 1 cup red wine
- 2 cups beef stock
- 2 tbsp butter, softened
- 2 celery stalks, chopped
- 1 tbsp fresh thyme
- 2 tbsp flour
- Salt and pepper to taste

Directions:

1. Rub the lamb with salt and pepper. Melt butter on Sauté and cook onions, celery, and garlic for 5 minutes. Add lamb and fry until browned for about 5-6 minutes. Dust the flour and stir. Pour in the stock and red wine. Seal the lid, and cook on High Pressure for 30 minutes. Do a natural release for 10 minutes. Serve with thyme.

Beef Goulash With Cabbage & Potatoes

Servings: 6
Cooking Time: 45 Minutes
Ingredients:

- 1 cup sun-dried tomatoes, diced
- 2 lb beef stew meat
- 3 potatoes, cut into chunks
- 1 onion, chopped
- 1 carrot, chopped
- 1 cabbage head, shredded
- 4 cups beef broth
- 3 tbsp tomato paste
- 1 tsp tabasco sauce
- Salt and pepper to taste
- 3 tbsp butter

Directions:

1. Melt the butter oil in your Instant Pot on Sauté and cook the onion until translucent for 2 minutes. Add the tomato paste and stir. Add the beef, tomatoes, potatoes, carrot, cabbage, broth, tabasco sauce, salt, and pepper and seal the lid. Cook on High Pressure for 35 minutes. Do a quick release.

Spicy Pork Sausage Ragu

Servings: 4

Cooking Time: 25 Minutes

Ingredients:

- 1 lb pork sausage, casings removed
- 2 tbsp olive oil
- 2 garlic cloves, minced
- 1 onion, chopped
- 1 cup chopped tomatoes
- ½ tsp oregano
- 1 tsp red chili flakes
- 1 cup chicken stock
- Salt and pepper to taste
- 2 tbsp parsley, chopped

Directions:

1. Warm the olive oil in your Instant Pot on Sauté. Place in garlic and onion and cook until fragrant. Add and brown the sausage for 8 minutes. Stir constantly, breaking the meat with a wooden spatula. Stir in chicken stock, red chili flakes, oregano, and chopped tomatoes and seal the lid. Select Manual and cook for 10 minutes on High.

2. When over, perform a quick pressure release and unlock the lid. Adjust seasoning to taste. Cook on Sauté until the sauce thickens. Top with parsley and serve.

Caribean-style Pork With Mango Sauce

Servings: 6

Cooking Time: 70 Minutes

Ingredients:

- 1 ½ tsp onion powder
- 1 tsp dried thyme
- Salt and pepper to taste
- 1 tsp cayenne pepper
- 1 tsp ground allspice
- ½ tsp ground nutmeg
- ½ tsp ground cinnamon
- 2 lb pork shoulder
- 1 mango, cut into chunks
- 1 tbsp olive oil
- ½ cup water
- 2 tbsp cilantro, minced

Directions:

1. In a bowl, combine onion, thyme, allspice, cinnamon, pepper, sea salt, cayenne, and nutmeg. Coat the pork with olive oil. Season with seasoning mixture. Warm oil on Sauté in your Instant Pot. Add in the pork and cook for 5 minutes until browned completely. To the pot, add water and mango chunks. Seal the lid, press Meat/Stew, and cook on High Pressure for 45 minutes.

2. Release the pressure naturally for 10 minutes. Transfer the pork to a cutting board to cool. To make the sauce, pour the cooking liquid into a food processor and pulse until smooth. Shred the pork and arrange it on a serving platter. Serve topped with mango salsa and cilantro.

Beef Ragù Bolognese

Servings: 4
Cooking Time: 40 Minutes
Ingredients:

- ½ cup Pecorino Romano cheese, shredded
- 1 lb ground beef
- 2 tbsp butter
- 1 onion, chopped
- 1 carrot, chopped
- 1 celery stalk, chopped
- Salt and pepper to taste
- 2 tbsp basil, chopped
- 1 tbsp red wine
- 16 oz tomato sauce
- 2 tbsp passata
- 16 oz fettuccine pasta

Directions:

1. In the Instant Pot, add the pasta and cover with salted water. Seal the lid, press Manual, and cook for 4 minutes on High. Once ready, do a quick pressure release. Drain the pasta and remove to a bowl; cover with foil to keep warm.
2. Melt the butter on Sauté. Add in onion, carrot, and celery. Cook for 3-4 minutes. Mix in the ground beef and brown for 8-10 minutes, stirring occasionally. Pour in red wine, tomato sauce, and passata, and season with salt and black pepper. Seal the lid and select Manual.
3. Cook for 10 minutes on High. When ready, do a quick pressure release. Carefully unlock the lid. Pour the Bolognese sauce over the pasta, sprinkle with Pecorino Romano cheese, and top with basil to serve.

Chinese Beef With Bok Choy

Servings: 4
Cooking Time: 45 Minutes
Ingredients:

- 1 lb stew beef meat, cubed
- 1 onion, quartered
- 1 garlic clove, minced
- 2 tbsp sesame oil
- 1 carrot, thinly chopped
- 1 tbsp rice wine
- 1 bok choy, sliced
- 12 oz broccoli florets
- 1 red chili, sliced
- 1 tsp ground ginger
- 1 cup beef broth
- ¼ cup soy sauce
- 2 tbsp fish sauce

Directions:

1. Warm the sesame oil in your Instant Pot on Sauté. Add in beef meat, onion, garlic, carrot, ginger, and red chili and cook for 5-6 minutes. Stir in beef broth, rice wine, soy sauce, and fish sauce and seal the lid. Select Manual and cook for 30 minutes on High pressure. When done, perform a quick pressure release. Put in broccoli and bok choy and cook for 4-5 minutes on Sauté. Serve.

Stewed Beef With Potatoes

Servings: 4
Cooking Time: 60 Minutes
Ingredients:

- 1 lb russet potatoes, cut into chunks
- 1 lb beef shoulder
- 2 carrots, chopped
- 1 onion, finely chopped
- 4 tbsp olive oil
- 2 tbsp tomato paste
- 1 tbsp flour
- 4 cups beef broth
- 1 celery stalk, chopped
- 1 tbsp parsley, chopped
- 1 cayenne pepper, chopped
- Salt and pepper to taste

Directions:

1. Warm oil on Sauté. Stir-fry onion, carrots, and potatoes for 7-8 minutes. Stir in flour and press Cancel. Add beef, tomato paste, broth, celery, parsley, cayenne pepper, salt, and pepper Seal the lid and cook on High Pressure for 40 minutes. Do a quick release.

Smoky Shredded Pork With White Beans

Servings: 4
Cooking Time: 65 Minutes
Ingredients:

- 2 lb pork shoulder, halved
- 2 tbsp vegetable oil
- 1 onion, chopped
- 1 cup vegetable broth
- 2 tbsp liquid smoke
- Salt and pepper to taste
- 1 cup cooked white beans
- 2 tbsp parsley, chopped

Directions:

1. Warm the vegetable oil in your Instant Pot on Sauté. Place in onion and cook for 3 minutes. Sprinkle pork shoulder with salt and pepper, add it to the pot and brown for 5 minutes on all sides. Pour in vegetable broth and liquid smoke and scrape any brown bits from the bottom. Seal the lid, select Manual, and cook for 35 minutes on High.

2. When ready, allow a natural release for 10 minutes, then perform a quick pressure release, and unlock the lid. Remove pork and shred it. Stir white beans in the pot and put shredded pork back. Top with parsley and serve.

Gruyere Mushroom & Mortadella Cups

Servings: 4
Cooking Time: 20 Minutes
Ingredients:

- 4 eggs, beaten
- 1 tsp olive oil
- ½ tsp paprika
- ½ cup mushrooms, chopped
- 1 cup mortadella, chopped
- 1 tbsp parsley, minced
- Salt and pepper to taste
- 2 tbsp Gruyere, grated

Directions:

1. Mix the eggs, olive oil, 1 tbsp of water, and paprika in a bowl. Add in mushrooms, parsley, salt, pepper, and mortadella. Divide the mixture between ramekins and top with Gruyere cheese.

2. Pour 1 cup of water into your Instant Pot and fit in a trivet. Place the ramekins on the trivet and seal the lid. Select Manual and cook for 12 minutes on High pressure. Once ready, perform a quick pressure release. Carefully unlock the lid. Serve warm.

Short Ribs With Red Wine & Cheese Sauce

Servings: 6
Cooking Time: 1 Hour
Ingredients:

- 3 lb beef short ribs
- Salt and pepper to taste
- 2 tbsp olive oil
- 1 onion, chopped
- 1 large carrot, chopped
- 1 celery stalk, chopped
- 3 garlic cloves, chopped
- 2 cups beef broth
- 14.5-oz can diced tomatoes
- ½ cup dry red wine
- ¼ cup red wine vinegar
- 2 bay leaves
- ¼ tsp red pepper flakes
- 2 tbsp chopped parsley
- ½ cup cheese cream

Directions:

1. Season short ribs with black pepper and salt. Warm olive oil on Sauté. Add in short ribs and sear for 3 minutes on each side until browned. Set aside on a bowl. Drain everything only to be left with 1 tbsp of the remaining fat from the pot. Stir-fry garlic, carrot, onion, and celery in the hot fat for 4-6 minutes until it was fragrant.
2. Stir in broth, wine, flakes, vinegar, tomatoes, bay leaves, and remaining pepper and salt. Set to Sauté and bring the mixture to a boil. With the bone-side up, lay short ribs into the braising liquid. Seal the lid and cook on High Pressure for 40 minutes.
3. Release the pressure quickly. Set the short ribs on a plate. Get rid of bay leaves. Skim and get rid of the fat from the surface of the braising liquid. Using an immersion blender, blitz the liquid for 1 minute. Add in cheese cream, pepper, and salt, and blend until smooth. Arrange the ribs onto a serving plate, pour the sauce over, and top with parsley. Serve.

Spiced Mexican Pork

Servings: 4
Cooking Time: 55 Minutes + Marinating Time
Ingredients:

- 2 lb pork shoulder, cut into chunks
- 1 chipotle pepper in adobo sauce, chopped
- 3 garlic cloves, minced
- 1 red onion, chopped
- ½ tsp ground coriander
- 1 tsp ground cumin
- 1 tbsp lime juice
- ¼ cup chile enchilada sauce
- 1 tsp Mexican oregano
- Salt and pepper to taste

Directions:

1. Place garlic, onion, ground coriander, cumin, lime juice, Mexican oregano, chipotle pepper, enchilada sauce, salt, pepper, and ½ cup of water in a blender and pulse until smooth. Place the mixture in a large bowl and add in pork chunks; toss to coat. Cover with cling foil and let marinate in the fridge for 30 minutes.
2. Next, remove from the fridge and transfer to your Instant Pot. Pour in ½ cup of water and seal the lid. Select Manual and cook for 25 minutes on High pressure. When ready, allow a natural release for 15 minutes and unlock the lid. Cook for 5 minutes on Sauté until the sauce thickens. Serve warm.

Poultry

Thyme Chicken With White Wine

Servings: 6
Cooking Time: 45 Minutes
Ingredients:

- 1 cup chicken stock
- ½ cup white wine
- ½ onion, chopped
- 2 cloves garlic, minced
- 3.5-pound whole chicken
- Salt and pepper to taste
- ½ tsp dried thyme
- 3 tbsp butter, melted
- ½ tsp paprika

Directions:

1. Into your Instant Pot, add onion, stock, wine, and garlic. Over the mixture, place a steamer rack. Rub pepper, salt, and thyme onto chicken. Put it on the rack breast-side up. Seal the lid, press Manual, and cook for 26 minutes. Release the pressure quickly. Preheat oven broiler. In a bowl, mix paprika and butter. Remove the chicken from your pot. Get rid of onion and stock. Brush butter mixture onto the chicken and cook under the broiler for 5 minutes until chicken skin is crispy and browned. Set chicken to a cutting board to cool for about 5 minutes, then carve, and transfer to a serving platter. Serve.

Sweet & Spicy Bbq Chicken

Servings: 4
Cooking Time: 35 Minutes
Ingredients:

- 6 chicken drumsticks
- 1 tbsp olive oil
- 1 onion, chopped
- 1 tsp garlic, minced
- 1 jalapeño pepper, minced
- ½ cup sweet BBQ sauce
- 1 tbsp arrowroot

Directions:

1. Warm the olive oil in your Instant Pot on Sauté. Add in the onion and cook for 3 minutes. Add in garlic and jalapeño pepper and cook for another minute. Stir in barbecue sauce and 1/2 cup of water. Put in chicken drumsticks and seal the lid. Select Manual and cook for 18 minutes on High pressure. When over, perform a quick pressure release and unlock the lid. Mix 2 tbsp of water and arrowroot and pour it into the pot. Cook for 5 minutes on Sauté until the liquid thickens. Top with sauce and serve.

Creamy Pesto Chicken

Servings:6
Cooking Time: 10 Minutes

Ingredients:

- ½ cup pesto
- ¾ cup heavy cream
- 1 tablespoon all-purpose flour
- 2 tablespoons grated Parmesan cheese
- 2 cloves garlic, peeled and minced
- ¼ teaspoon salt
- ½ teaspoon ground black pepper
- 3 pounds boneless and skinless chicken thighs
- 1 cup water

Directions:

1. In a medium bowl, whisk together pesto, cream, flour, cheese, garlic, salt, and pepper.
2. Add chicken to a 7-cup glass baking dish. Pour pesto mixture over chicken.
3. Add water to the Instant Pot and insert steam rack. Place glass baking dish on steam rack. Lock lid.
4. Press the Manual or Pressure Cook button and adjust time to 10 minutes. When timer beeps, let pressure release naturally for 10 minutes. Quick-release any additional pressure until float valve drops. Unlock lid. Check chicken using a meat thermometer to ensure internal temperature is at least 165°F.
5. Carefully remove dish from pot. Serve warm.

Lemon Chicken Wings

Servings: 4
Cooking Time: 20 Minutes

Ingredients:

- 2 tbsp olive oil
- 8 chicken wings
- ½ tsp chili powder
- ½ tsp garlic powder
- ½ tsp onion powder
- ½ tsp cayenne pepper
- Salt and pepper to taste
- ½ cup chicken broth
- 2 lemons, juiced

Directions:

1. Coat the chicken wings with olive oil. Season with chili powder, onion powder, salt, garlic powder, cayenne, and pepper. In your Instant Pot, add the wings and chicken broth. Seal the lid and cook on High Pressure for 4 minutes. Do a quick pressure release.
2. Preheat the oven to 380 F. Onto a greased baking sheet, place the wings in a single layer and drizzle over the lemon juice. Bake for 5 minutes until the skin is crispy.

Tuscan Vegetable Chicken Stew

Servings: 4
Cooking Time: 60 Minutes
Ingredients:

- 14 oz broccoli and cauliflower florets
- A handful of yellow wax beans, whole
- 1 whole chicken
- 1 onion, peeled, chopped
- 1 potato, peeled, chopped
- 3 carrots, chopped
- 1 tomato, peeled, chopped
- ¼ cup extra virgin olive oil
- Salt and pepper to taste

Directions:

1. Warm 3 tbsp olive oil in your Instant Pot on Sauté. Stir-fry the onion for 3-4 minutes on Sauté. Add the carrots and sauté for 5 more minutes. Add the remaining oil, broccoli, potato, wax beans, tomato, salt, and pepper and top with chicken. Add 1 cup of water and seal the lid. Cook on High Pressure for 30 minutes. Release the pressure naturally for about 10 minutes. Carefully unlock the lid. Serve warm.

Delicious Turkey Burgers

Servings: 4
Cooking Time: 35 Minutes
Ingredients:

- 1 lb ground turkey
- 2 egg
- 1 tbsp flour
- 1 onion, finely chopped
- Salt and pepper to taste
- 1 tbsp sour cream

Directions:

1. In a bowl, add ground turkey, egg, flour, onion, salt, pepper, and sour cream and mix well. Form the mixture into patties. Line parchment paper over a baking dish and arrange the patties. Pour 1 cup of water into your Instant Pot. Lay the trivet and place the baking dish on top.
2. Seal the lid. Cook on Manual for 15 minutes on High. Release the pressure naturally for 10 minutes. Unlock the lid. Serve with lettuce and tomatoes.

Chicken & Vegetable Stew

Servings: 4
Cooking Time: 45 Minutes
Ingredients:

- 2 cups fire-roasted tomatoes, diced
- ½ cup button mushrooms, sliced
- 1 lb chicken breasts, chopped
- 1 tbsp fresh basil, chopped
- 2 cups coconut milk
- 1 cup chicken broth
- Salt and pepper to taste
- 2 tbsp tomato paste
- 2 celery stalks, chopped
- 2 carrots, chopped
- 2 tbsp coconut oil
- 1 onion, finely chopped

Directions:

1. Warm the coconut oil in your Instant Pot on Sauté. Add celery, onion, and carrots and cook for 7 minutes, stirring constantly. Add tomato paste, basil, and mushrooms. Continue to cook for 10 more minutes. Addin the tomatoes, chicken, coconut milk, chicken broth, salt, and pepper. Seal the lid and cook on Manual for 15 minutes on High. Do a quick release. Serve warm.

Simple Whole Chicken

Servings:4
Cooking Time: 25 Minutes
Ingredients:

- 1 whole chicken
- 2 teaspoons sea salt
- 1 teaspoon ground black pepper
- 1 medium apple, peeled, quartered, and cored
- 1 medium onion, peeled and roughly chopped
- 3 cloves garlic, halved
- 1 celery stalk, chopped
- 2 large carrots, peeled and chopped
- 3 sprigs thyme
- 2 cups water

Directions:

1. Pat the chicken dry, inside and out, with paper towels. Sprinkle chicken with salt and pepper, then place the apple in the cavity of the bird.
2. In the bottom of the Instant Pot, scatter the onion, garlic, celery, carrots, and thyme. Pour in the water. Place the trivet over the vegetables.
3. Place chicken on the trivet. Lock lid.
4. Press the Manual button and adjust time to 25 minutes. When timer beeps, let pressure release naturally until float valve drops and then unlock lid. Check the chicken using a meat thermometer to ensure the internal temperature is at least 165°F.
5. Remove chicken and vegetables. Discard apple. Serve warm.

Tasty Chicken Breasts With Bbq Sauce

Servings: 6
Cooking Time: 20 Minutes
Ingredients:

- 2 lb chicken breasts
- 1 tsp salt
- 1 ½ cups barbecue sauce
- 1 small onion, minced
- 1 cup carrots, chopped
- 4 garlic cloves

Directions:

1. Rub salt onto the chicken and place it in the Instant Pot. Add onion, carrots, garlic, and barbeque sauce; toss to coat. Seal the lid, press Manual, and cook on High for 15 minutes. Do a quick release. Shred the chicken and stir into the sauce. Serve.

Rosemary Chicken With Asparagus Sauce

Servings: 4
Cooking Time: 40 Minutes
Ingredients:

- 1 whole chicken
- 4 garlic cloves, minced
- 2 tbsp olive oil
- 4 fresh thyme, minced
- 3 fresh rosemary, minced
- 2 lemons, zested, quartered
- Salt and pepper to taste
- 2 tbsp olive oil

- 8 oz asparagus, chopped
- 1 onion, chopped
- 1 cup chicken stock
- 1 tbsp soy sauce
- 1 fresh thyme sprig
- 1 tbsp flour
- Chopped parsley to garnish

Directions:

1. Rub all sides of the chicken with garlic, rosemary, black pepper, lemon zest, thyme, and salt. Into the chicken cavity, insert lemon wedges. Warm the olive oil on Sauté in your Instant Pot. Add in onion and asparagus, and sauté for 5 minutes until softened. Mix chicken stock, thyme sprig, black pepper, soy sauce, and salt. Into the inner pot, set trivet over asparagus mixture.

2. On top of the trivet, place the chicken with breast-side up. Seal the lid, select Manual, and cook for 20 minutes on High. Do a quick release. Remove the chicken to a serving platter. In the inner pot, sprinkle flour over asparagus mixture and blend the sauce with an immersion blender until desired consistency. Top the chicken with asparagus sauce and garnish with parsley.

Chicken Paprikash

Servings: 4
Cooking Time: 25 Minutes
Ingredients:

- 2 tablespoons ghee
- 1 medium onion, peeled and diced
- 1 small green bell pepper, seeded and diced
- 4 cloves garlic, minced
- 4 skin-on chicken breast halves
- 1 large tomato, diced
- ¼ cup tomato sauce
- 2 tablespoons Hungarian paprika
- 1 cup chicken broth
- 1 tablespoon flour
- ¾ cup sour cream
- ½ teaspoon sea salt
- ¼ teaspoon ground black pepper

Directions:

1. Press the Sauté button on the Instant Pot and heat ghee. Add onion and green pepper and sauté for 3–5 minutes until onions are translucent. Stir in garlic. Add the chicken breast skin-side down and brown for 3–4 minutes. Sprinkle the diced tomato over the chicken.

2. In a medium bowl, whisk together tomato sauce, paprika, and chicken broth. Pour over chicken. Lock lid.

3. Press the Poultry button and cook for the default time of 15 minutes. When timer beeps, let pressure release naturally for 10 minutes. Quick-release any additional pressure until float valve drops and then unlock lid. Check the chicken using a meat thermometer to ensure the internal temperature is at least 165°F. Transfer chicken to a serving platter.

4. Whisk flour and sour cream into the juices in the Instant Pot. Press the Sauté button, press the Adjust button to change the temperature to Less, and simmer unlidded for 5 minutes until sauce thickens. Season with salt and pepper. Pour sauce over chicken and serve warm.

Sticky Chicken Wings

Servings: 6

Cooking Time: 35 Minutes + Marinating Time

Ingredients:

- 2 lb chicken wings
- 3 tbsp light brown sugar
- 2 tbsp soy sauce
- 1 small lime, juiced
- ½ tsp sea salt
- 1 tsp five-spice powder

Directions:

1. Combine soy sauce, lime juice, five-spice powder, brown sugar, and salt in a bowl. Place chicken wing and marinade in a resealable bag and shake it. Transfer to the fridge and let marinate for 30 minutes.

2. Pour 1/2 cup of water and marinate chicken wings with the juices in your Instant Pot. Seal the lid, select Manual, and cook for 15 minutes on High pressure. When done, allow a natural release for 10 minutes and unlock the lid. Cook on Sauté until the sauce thickens. Serve.

Asian Sesame Chicken

Servings:6

Cooking Time: 25 Minutes

Ingredients:

- ¼ cup coconut aminos
- ¼ cup tomato sauce
- ½ cup honey
- 2 teaspoons fish sauce
- 1 teaspoon hot sauce
- ¼ teaspoon white pepper
- 2 pounds boneless chicken thighs, cut into 1" cubes
- 1 tablespoon sesame oil
- 1 small onion, peeled and diced
- 3 cloves garlic, minced
- 1 tablespoon arrowroot powder
- 1 tablespoon water
- 3 green onions, sliced (white and green parts)
- 1 tablespoon toasted sesame seeds

Directions:

1. In a medium bowl, whisk together coconut aminos, tomato sauce, honey, fish sauce, hot sauce, and white pepper. Toss chicken to coat. Set aside in the refrigerator.

2. Press the Sauté button on the Instant Pot and heat sesame oil. Add onion and garlic and sauté for about 3–5 minutes until onions are translucent. Add chicken and all of the sauce into the onion mixture. Toss to coat. Lock lid.

3. Press the Poultry button and cook for the default time of 15 minutes. When timer beeps, let pressure release naturally for 10 minutes. Quick-release any additional pressure until float valve drops and then unlock lid. Check the chicken using a meat thermometer to ensure the internal temperature is at least 165°F. Using a slotted spoon, transfer chicken to a serving platter.

4. In a small bowl, whisk together arrowroot powder and water to create a slurry. Stir this into sauce in the Instant Pot. Press the Sauté button, press the Adjust button to change the temperature to Less, and simmer unlidded for 5 minutes to thicken the sauce.

5. Pour desired amount of sauce over chicken and garnish with sliced green onions and sesame seeds.

Chili & Lemon Chicken Wings

Servings: 4
Cooking Time: 20 Minutes
Ingredients:

- 1 lb chicken wings
- 2 tbsp olive oil
- 1 tbsp honey
- 1 lemon, zested and juiced
- ½ tsp garlic powder
- ½ tsp cayenne pepper
- ½ chili pepper, chopped
- Salt and pepper to taste
- 1 ½ cups chicken broth

Directions:

1. Combine olive oil, lemon zest, lemon juice, red chili pepper, honey, garlic powder, cayenne pepper, black pepper, and salt in a bowl. Brush chicken wings with the mixture on all sides. Place the chicken broth and chicken wings in your Instant Pot. Seal the lid, select Manual, and cook for 10 minutes on High pressure. When over, perform a quick pressure release. Serve warm.

Sage Turkey & Red Wine Casserole

Servings: 4
Cooking Time: 50 Minutes
Ingredients:

- 1 lb boneless turkey breast, cubed
- 1 onion, sliced
- 1 celery stalk, sliced
- 2 tbsp olive oil
- 1 carrot, diced
- ½ cup red wine
- Salt and pepper to taste
- 1 cup chicken broth
- 1 tbsp tomato puree
- 2 tbsp sage, chopped

Directions:

1. Warm olive oil in your IP on Sauté. Add in the turkey cubes and brown for 4-5 minutes, stirring occasionally; set aside. Add onion, celery, and carrot to the pot and sauté for 3-4 minutes. Stir in tomato puree, red wine, salt, and pepper and pour in chicken broth. Stir and return the turkey. Seal the lid, select Manual, and cook for 20 minutes on High. Once ready, release pressure naturally for 10 minutes. Unlock the lid, top with sage and serve.

Feta Cheese Turkey Balls

Servings: 6
Cooking Time: 35 Minutes
Ingredients:

- 1 onion, minced
- ½ cup plain bread crumbs
- 1/3 cup feta, crumbled
- Salt and pepper to taste
- ½ tsp dried oregano
- 1 lb ground turkey
- 1 egg, lightly beaten
- 1 tbsp olive oil
- 1 carrot, minced
- ½ celery stalk, minced
- 3 cups tomato puree
- 2 cups water

Directions:

1. In a mixing bowl, combine half the onion, oregano, turkey, salt, crumbs, pepper, and egg, and stir until everything is well incorporated. Heat oil on Sauté in your Instant Pot. Cook celery, remaining onion, and carrot for 5 minutes until soft. Pour in water and tomato puree. Adjust the seasonings. Roll the mixture into meatballs, and drop into the sauce. Seal the lid. Press Meat/Stew and cook on High Pressure for 5 minutes. Release the pressure naturally for 20 minutes. Serve topped with feta.

Jamaican Chicken With Pineapple Sauce

Servings: 4

Cooking Time: 40 Minutes

Ingredients:

- 1 lb chicken thighs
- ½ cup coconut cream
- 2 tbsp soy sauce
- 1 cup pineapple chunks
- 1 tsp Jamaican seasoning
- 1 tsp coriander seeds
- ¼ tsp salt
- ½ cup cilantro, chopped
- 1 tsp arrowroot starch

Directions:

1. Place chicken thighs, coconut cream, soy sauce, Jamaican jerk seasoning, coriander seeds, and salt in your Instant Pot and stir. Pour in 1 cup of water and seal the lid; cook for 15 minutes on manual. Once over, allow a natural release for 10 minutes and unlock the lid.
2. Remove chicken to a bowl. Combine arrowroot starch and 1 tbsp of water in a cup and pour it into the pot. Add in pineapple chunks and cook for 4-5 minutes on Sauté. Top the chicken with cilantro and sauce. Serve.

Corn & Sweet Potato Soup With Chicken

Servings: 4

Cooking Time: 25 Minutes

Ingredients:

- 4 oz canned diced green chiles, drained
- 2 chicken breasts, diced
- 2 garlic cloves, minced
- 1 cup chicken stock
- 1 cup corn kernels
- 1 sweet potato, peeled, cubed
- 2 tsp chili powder
- 1 tsp ground cumin
- 2 cups cheddar, shredded
- 2 cups creme fraiche
- Salt and pepper to taste
- Cilantro leaves, chopped

Directions:

1. Add chicken, corn, chili powder, cumin, chicken stock, sweet potato, green chiles, and garlic to your Instant Pot. Mix well. Seal the lid and cook on High Pressure for 10 minutes. Release the pressure quickly. Set the chicken to a cutting board and shred it. Return to the pot and stir well into the liquid. Stir in cheese and creme fraiche; Season with pepper and salt. Cook for 2-3 minutes until the cheese is melted. Place chowder into plates and top with cilantro. Serve warm.

Greek Chicken With Potatoes & Okra

Servings: 4
Cooking Time: 45 Minutes
Ingredients:

- 2 lb chicken thighs, skinless and boneless
- 1 lb potatoes, peeled and cut into quarters
- 2 tbsp olive oil
- ¾ cup chicken stock
- ¼ lb okra, tops removed
- ¼ cup lemon juice
- 2 tbsp Greek seasoning
- Salt and pepper to taste

Directions:

1. Warm the olive oil in your Instant Pot on Sauté. Sprinkle chicken thighs with salt and pepper. Place in the pot and cook for 6 minutes on all sides. Combine chicken stock, lemon juice, and Greek seasoning in a bowl and pour over the chicken. Stir in potatoes, okra, salt, and pepper and seal the lid. Select Manual and cook for 15 minutes on High pressure. Once ready, allow a natural release for 10 minutes and unlock the lid. Serve warm.

Chicken Breast Parmesan With Mushrooms

Servings:8
Cooking Time: 20 Minutes
Ingredients:

- ½ cup all-purpose flour
- ½ teaspoon salt
- ½ teaspoon ground black pepper
- 2 pounds boneless, skinless chicken breast, cut in 1" cubes
- 2 tablespoons olive oil
- 1 large onion, peeled and diced
- 1 tablespoon Italian seasoning
- 2 tablespoons tomato paste
- ½ cup chicken broth
- 1 can tomato sauce
- 1 teaspoon balsamic vinegar
- 2 cups sliced white mushrooms
- 2 teaspoons honey
- 2 tablespoons chopped fresh parsley
- 1 cup grated Parmesan cheese

Directions:

1. Add the flour, salt, and pepper to a large zip-closure bag; seal and shake to mix. Add chicken cubes to the bag, seal, and shake to coat the meat in the flour.
2. Press the Sauté button on the Instant Pot. Heat the oil and add the chicken and onion. Stir-fry for 3–5 minutes until onions are translucent. Stir in Italian seasoning and tomato paste. Sauté for 2 minutes. Stir in the broth, tomato sauce, vinegar, mushrooms, and honey. Lock lid.
3. Press the Manual button and adjust time to 12 minutes. When timer beeps, let pressure release naturally for 10 minutes. Quick-release any additional pressure until float valve drops and then unlock lid. Check the chicken using a meat thermometer to ensure the internal temperature is at least 165°F.
4. Stir the cooked chicken and sauce in the Instant Pot. Transfer to a serving dish. Garnish with parsley and grated Parmesan cheese and serve warm.

Chicken & Pepper Cacciatore

Servings: 4
Cooking Time: 50 Minutes
Ingredients:

- 4 chicken thighs, with the bone, skin removed
- 3 mixed bell peppers, cut into strips
- 2 tbsp olive oil
- Salt and pepper to taste
- 2 garlic cloves, minced
- 1 diced onion
- 1 cup canned diced tomatoes
- 2 tbsp chopped rosemary
- ½ tsp oregano
- 10 black olives, pitted

Directions:

1. Warm olive oil in your Instant Pot on Sauté. Sprinkle chicken with salt and pepper and cook in the pot for 2-3 minutes per side; reserve. Add bell pepper, garlic, and onion to the pot and cook for 5 minutes. Stir in tomatoes, oregano, and 1 cup water and return the chicken. Seal the lid, select Manual, and cook for 20 minutes on High pressure. When done, allow a natural release for 10 minutes and unlock the lid. Serve topped with black olives and rosemary.

Island Chicken Legs

Servings:5
Cooking Time: 21 Minutes
Ingredients:

- 1 can pineapple, including juice
- 2 tablespoons tomato paste
- ¼ cup granulated sugar
- 2 tablespoons soy sauce
- 2 teaspoons grated fresh ginger
- 1 teaspoon garlic salt
- 3 pounds chicken legs/drumsticks
- 1 cup water

Directions:

1. In a blender, combine pineapple, tomato paste, sugar, soy sauce, ginger, and garlic salt. Divide sauce in half. Add chicken legs to half of mixture and refrigerate 30 minutes.
2. Preheat oven to broiler at 500°F.
3. Add water to the Instant Pot and insert steam rack. Arrange chicken standing up, meaty side down, on steam rack. Lock lid.
4. Press the Poultry button and cook for the default time of 15 minutes. When timer beeps, let pressure release naturally for 5 minutes. Quick-release any additional pressure until float valve drops. Unlock lid. Check chicken using a meat thermometer to ensure internal temperature is at least 165°F.
5. Place chicken legs on a parchment paper–lined baking sheet and broil 3 minutes on each side to crisp chicken. Toss chicken in remaining sauce mixture.
6. Transfer chicken to a platte. Serve warm.

Fish & Seafood

Steamed Salmon Over Creamy Polenta

Servings: 4
Cooking Time: 30 Minutes
Ingredients:

- 4 salmon fillets, skin removed
- 1 cup corn grits polenta
- ½ cup coconut milk
- 3 cups chicken stock
- 3 tbsp butter
- Salt to taste
- 3 tbsp Cajun seasoning
- 1 tbsp sugar

Directions:
1. Combine polenta, milk, chicken stock, butter, and salt in the pot. In a bowl, mix Cajun seasoning, sugar, and salt. Oil the fillets with cooking spray and brush with the spice mixture. Insert a trivet in the pot and arrange the fillets on top. Seal the lid and cook on High Pressure for 9 minutes. Do a natural pressure release for 10 minutes.

Rosemary Cod With Cherry Tomatoes

Servings: 4
Cooking Time: 25 Minutes
Ingredients:

- 1 ½ lb cod fillets
- 3 tbsp butter
- 1 onion, sliced
- 2 garlic cloves, minced
- ½ lb cherry tomatoes, halved
- 1 lemon juice
- Salt and pepper to taste
- 2 tbsp rosemary, chopped
- 1 cup vegetable broth

Directions:
1. Melt the butter in your Instant Pot on Sauté. Add in the onion, garlic, and rosemary and sauté for 3 minutes, stirring often. Add in the cod fillets and cook for 3-4 minutes on both sides. Sprinkle with salt and pepper, and cook for 3-4 minutes. Pour in vegetable broth and top with cherry tomatoes. Seal the lid, select Manual. Cook for 3 minutes on High pressure. When ready, perform a quick pressure release and unlock the lid. Top the cod with lemon juice and serve with sauce.

Teriyaki Salmon

Servings:2
Cooking Time: 5 Minutes
Ingredients:

- 2 salmon fillets
- ½ teaspoon salt
- 2 tablespoons teriyaki sauce
- 1 cup water
- 1 teaspoon toasted sesame seeds
- 2 tablespoons sliced green onion (greens only)

Directions:
1. Pat fillets dry with a paper towel and place in a steamer basket. Season salmon with salt. Brush teriyaki sauce on tops of salmon.
2. Add water to the Instant Pot and insert steam rack. Place steamer basket on steam rack. Lock lid.
3. Press the Manual or Pressure Cook button and adjust time to 5 minutes. When timer beeps, quick-release pressure until float valve drops. Unlock lid.
4. Transfer fish to plates and garnish with sesame seeds and onion greens. Serve immediately.

Seafood Medley With Rosemary Rice

Servings: 4

Cooking Time: 45 Minutes

Ingredients:

- 1 lb frozen seafood mix
- 1 cup brown rice
- 1 tbsp calamari ink
- 2 tbsp extra virgin olive oil
- 2 garlic cloves, crushed
- 1 tbsp chopped rosemary
- ½ tsp salt
- 3 cups fish stock
- ½ lemon

Directions:

1. Add in seafood mix, rice, calamari ink, olive oil, garlic, rosemary, salt, stock, and lemon, seal the lid and cook on Manual for 25 minutes on High. Release the pressure naturally for 10 minutes. Squeeze lemon juice and serve.

Thyme For Lemon-butter Sea Bass

Servings:2

Cooking Time: 7 Minutes

Ingredients:

- 2 tablespoons unsalted butter, melted
- 1 tablespoon lemon juice
- 2 teaspoons fresh thyme leaves
- ¼ cup Italian bread crumbs
- 2 sea bass fillets
- ½ teaspoon salt
- ¼ teaspoon ground black pepper
- 1 cup water

Directions:

1. In a small bowl, combine butter, lemon juice, thyme, and bread crumbs to form a thick paste.
2. Pat sea bass fillets dry with a paper towel. Season sea bass with salt and pepper. Press paste on top of each fillet and place in steamer basket.
3. Add water to the Instant Pot and insert steam rack. Place basket on steam rack. Lock lid.
4. Press the Manual or Pressure Cook button and adjust time to 5 minutes. When timer beeps, quick-release pressure until float valve drops. Unlock lid.
5. Line a baking sheet with parchment paper. Transfer fillets to prepared baking sheet. Broil approximately 1–2 minutes until tops are browned.
6. Remove from heat. Serve warm.

Herby Crab Legs With Lemon

Servings: 4

Cooking Time: 10 Minutes

Ingredients:

- 3 lb king crab legs, broken in half
- 1 tsp rosemary
- 1 tsp thyme
- 1 tsp dill
- ¼ cup butter, melted
- Salt and pepper to taste
- 1 lemon, cut into wedges

Directions:

1. Pour 1 cup of water into your Instant Pot and fit in a trivet. Season the crab legs with rosemary, thyme, dill, salt, and pepper; place on the trivet. Seal the lid, select Manual, and cook for 3 minutes. When ready, perform a quick pressure release. Remove crab legs to a bowl and drizzle with melted butter. Serve with lemon wedges.

Tangy Shrimp Curry

Servings: 4
Cooking Time: 15 Minutes
Ingredients:
- 1 lb shrimp, deveined
- 2 tbsp sesame oil
- 1 onion, chopped
- ½ tsp fresh ginger, grated
- 1 garlic clove, minced
- 1 tsp cayenne pepper
- 1 tbsp lime juice
- 1 cup coconut milk
- 1 tbsp curry powder
- Salt and pepper to taste

Directions:
1. Heat the sesame oil in your Instant Pot on Sauté and cook the onion, garlic, and ginger for 3-4 minutes. Stir in curry powder, cayenne pepper, salt, and pepper and cook for 3 minutes. Pour in coconut milk, shrimp, and 1 cup of water and seal the lid. Select Manual and cook for 4 minutes on Low pressure. Once done, perform a quick pressure release. Drizzle with lime juice and serve.

Beer-steamed Shrimp

Servings:4
Cooking Time: 0 Minutes
Ingredients:
- 1 bottle beer
- 2 pounds jumbo shrimp, peeled and deveined
- 1 medium lemon, quartered
- 2 tablespoons Old Bay Seasoning

Directions:
1. Add beer to the Instant Pot and insert steamer basket. Place shrimp in basket. Squeeze lemons over shrimp and add squeezed wedges for additional aromatics. Lock lid.
2. Press the Steam button and adjust time to 0 minutes. When timer beeps, quick-release pressure until float valve drops. Unlock lid. Discard lemons.
3. Transfer shrimp to a serving dish and toss with Old Bay Seasoning. Serve warm or chilled.

Steamed Clams

Servings:4
Cooking Time: 10 Minutes
Ingredients:
- 2 pounds fresh clams, rinsed and purged
- 1 tablespoon olive oil
- 1 small white onion, peeled and diced
- 1 clove garlic, quartered
- ½ cup chardonnay
- ½ cup water

Directions:
1. Place clams in the steamer basket. Set aside.
2. Press the Sauté button on Instant Pot. Heat olive oil. Add onion and sauté 3–5 minutes until translucent. Add garlic and cook another minute. Pour in white wine and water. Insert steamer basket. Lock lid.
3. Press the Manual button and adjust time to 4 minutes. When the timer beeps, quick-release pressure until lid unlocks.
4. Transfer clams to four serving bowls and top with a generous scoop of cooking liquid.

Tuna & Veggie Egg Mix

Servings: 4
Cooking Time: 25 Minutes
Ingredients:

- 2 cans tuna, drained
- 1 carrot, chopped
- 10 oz broccoli, chopped
- 1 diced onion
- 2 eggs, beaten
- 1 can cream of celery soup
- ½ cup vegetable broth
- ¾ cup milk
- 2 tbsp butter
- ½ tsp oregano
- ½ rosemary
- Salt and pepper to taste

Directions:

1. Stir the tuna, carrot, broccoli, onion, eggs, celery soup, vegetable broth, milk, butter, oregano, rosemary, salt, and pepper in your Instant Pot and seal the lid. Select Manual and cook for 15 minutes on High. Perform a quick pressure release.

Spicy Salmon With Oregano & Sea Salt

Servings: 4
Cooking Time: 50 Minutes
Ingredients:

- 1 lb fresh salmon fillets, skin on
- ¼ cup olive oil
- ½ cup lemon juice
- 2 garlic cloves, crushed
- 1 tbsp oregano, chopped
- 1 tsp sea salt
- ¼ tsp chili flakes
- 2 cups fish stock

Directions:

1. In a bowl, mix oil, lemon juice, garlic, oregano leaves, salt, and flakes. Brush the fillets with the mixture and refrigerate for 30 minutes. Pour the stock in, and insert the trivet. Pat dry the salmon and place it on the steamer rack. Seal the lid, and cook on Steam for 10 minutes on High. Do a quick release and serve.

Corn & Mackerel Chowder

Servings: 4
Cooking Time: 45 Minutes
Ingredients:

- 6 oz mackerel fillets
- ½ cup wheat groats, soaked
- ½ cup kidney beans, soaked
- ¼ cup sweet corn
- 1 lb tomatoes, chopped
- 4 cups fish stock
- 4 tbsp olive oil
- 2 garlic cloves, crushed

Directions:

1. Heat olive oil on Sauté. Stir-fry tomatoes and garlic for 5 minutes. Add in stock, corn, kidney beans, and wheat groats. Seal the lid and cook on High Pressure for 25 minutes. Do a quick release. Add mackerel fillets. Seal the lid and cook on Steam for 8 minutes on High. Do a quick release. Serve.

Almond-crusted Salmon Fillets

Servings: 2
Cooking Time: 25 Minutes
Ingredients:

- 2 salmon fillets
- ½ cup olive oil
- Salt to taste
- ¼ cup flour
- 1 egg, beaten
- ¼ cup almonds, ground
- 2 tbsp dill, chopped

Directions:

1. Warm the olive oil in your Instant Pot on Sauté. Sprinkle salmon with salt. Dip it in the flour, then in beaten eggs, and finally in almonds. Put them in the pot and cook on both sides until browned. Set aside. Pour 1 cup of water into your Instant Pot; fit in a trivet. Place the salmon on the trivet and seal the lid. Select Manual and cook for 4 minutes on High. When done, allow a natural release for 10 minutes and unlock the lid. Serve sprinkled with dill.

Mediterranean Cod With Cherry Tomatoes

Servings: 4
Cooking Time: 20 Minutes
Ingredients:

- 1 lb cherry tomatoes, halved
- 1 bunch fresh thyme sprigs
- 4 fillets cod
- 2 tbsp olive oil
- 1 clove garlic, pressed
- Salt and pepper to taste
- 1 cup white rice
- 1 cup kalamata olives
- 2 tbsp pickled capers

Directions:

1. Line a parchment paper on the basket of the pot. Place about half the tomatoes in a single layer on the paper. Sprinkle with thyme, reserving some for garnish. Arrange cod fillets on top. Sprinkle with some olive oil. Spread the garlic, pepper, salt, and remaining tomatoes over the fish. In the pot, mix rice and 2 cups of water. Lay a trivet over the rice and water.
2. Lower steamer basket onto the trivet. Seal the lid, and cook for 7 minutes on Low Pressure. Release the pressure quickly. Remove the steamer basket and trivet from the pot. Use a fork to fluff the rice. Plate the fish fillets and apply a garnish of olives, reserved thyme, remaining olive oil, and capers. Serve with rice.

Mahi-mahi With A Lemon-caper Butter Sauce

Servings:2
Cooking Time: 7 Minutes
Ingredients:

- 2 mahi-mahi fillets
- 2 tablespoons fresh lemon juice
- 2 tablespoons capers
- 1 teaspoon sea salt
- 1 teaspoon lemon zest
- 2 tablespoons butter, cut into 2 pats
- 1 tablespoon chopped fresh parsley

Directions:

1. Place a piece of foil on the Instant Pot's steamer basket. Set both fillets on the foil. Create a "boat" with the foil by bringing up the edges. Pour lemon juice on fish. Add capers. Season fish with salt and zest. Add a pat of butter to each fillet. Set trivet in the Instant Pot and place the steamer basket on the trivet. Lock lid.
2. Press the Manual button and adjust time to 7 minutes. Quick-release pressure until float valve drops and then unlock lid.
3. Transfer fish to two plates. Garnish each with ½ tablespoon chopped parsley.

Paprika Catfish With Fresh Tarragon

Servings:2
Cooking Time: 3 Minutes
Ingredients:

- 1 can diced tomatoes, including juice
- 2 teaspoons dried minced onion
- ¼ teaspoon onion powder
- 1 teaspoon dried minced garlic
- ¼ teaspoon garlic powder
- 2 teaspoons smoked paprika
- 1 tablespoon chopped fresh tarragon
- 1 medium green bell pepper, seeded and diced
- 1 stalk celery, finely diced
- 1 teaspoon salt
- ¼ teaspoon ground black pepper
- 1 pound catfish fillets, rinsed and cut into bite-sized pieces

Directions:

1. Add all ingredients except fish to the Instant Pot and stir to mix. Once mixed, add the fish on top. Lock lid.
2. Press the Manual button and adjust time to 3 minutes. When timer beeps, quick-release pressure until float valve drops and then unlock lid.
3. Transfer all ingredients to a serving bowl. Serve warm.

Trout In Herb Sauce

Servings:4
Cooking Time: 5 Minutes
Ingredients:

- Trout
- 4 (½-pound) fresh river trout
- 1 teaspoon sea salt
- 4 cups torn lettuce leaves, divided
- 1 teaspoon white wine vinegar
- ½ cup water
- Herb Sauce
- ½ cup minced fresh flat-leaf parsley
- 2 teaspoons Italian seasoning
- 1 small shallot, peeled and minced
- 2 tablespoons mayonnaise
- ½ teaspoon fresh lemon juice
- ¼ teaspoon sugar
- Pinch of salt
- 2 tablespoons sliced almonds, toasted

Directions:

1. For Trout: Rinse the trout inside and out; pat dry. Sprinkle with salt inside and out. Put 3 cups lettuce leaves in the bottom of the Instant Pot. Arrange the trout over the top of the lettuce and top fish with the remaining lettuce.
2. Pour vinegar and water into pot. Lock lid.
3. Press the Manual button and adjust time to 3 minutes. When the timer beeps, let pressure release naturally for 3 minutes. Quick-release any additional pressure until float valve drops and then unlock lid.
4. Transfer fish to a serving plate. Peel and discard the skin from the fish. Remove and discard the heads if desired.
5. For Herb Sauce: In a small bowl, mix together the parsley, Italian seasoning, shallot, mayonnaise, lemon juice, sugar, and salt. Evenly divide among the fish, spreading it over them. Sprinkle toasted almonds over the top of the sauce. Serve.

Tilapia With Basil Pesto & Rice

Servings: 2
Cooking Time: 15 Minutes
Ingredients:
- 2 tilapia fillets
- 2 tbsp basil pesto
- ½ cup basmati rice
- Salt and pepper to taste

Directions:
1. Place the rice and 1 cup of water in your Instant Pot and season with salt and pepper; fit in a trivet. Place tilapia fillets in the middle of a parchment paper sheet. Top each fillet with pesto and roll all the edges to form a packet. Place it on the trivet and seal the lid.
2. Select Manual and cook for 6 minutes on Low pressure. Once ready, perform a quick pressure release. Carefully unlock the lid. Fluff the rice with a fork and transfer to a plate. Top with tilapia and serve.

Buttery Cod With Scallions

Servings: 4
Cooking Time: 15 Minutes
Ingredients:
- 4 cod fillets
- 1 fennel bulb, sliced
- Salt and pepper to taste
- 2 tbsp scallions, chopped
- 1 lemon, cut into wedges
- 1 tbsp garlic powder
- 2 tbsp butter, melted

Directions:
1. Pour 1 cup of water into your Instant Pot; fit in a trivet. Brush the cod fillets with butter and season with garlic, salt, and pepper. Place them on the trivet and top with fennel slices. Seal the lid, Select Manual, and cook for 5 minutes on High. Once ready, perform a quick pressure release. Sprinkle with scallions and serve with lemon wedges.

Stewed Cod And Peppers

Servings:2
Cooking Time: 3 Minutes
Ingredients:
- 1 can fire-roasted diced tomatoes, including juice
- ½ cup chicken broth
- 2 teaspoons smoked paprika
- 1 medium green bell pepper, seeded and diced small
- ½ cup diced yellow onion
- 1 teaspoon garlic salt
- ¼ teaspoon ground black pepper
- 1 pound cod fillets, cut into bite-sized pieces

Directions:
1. Place all ingredients except cod in the Instant Pot and stir. Once mixed, add fish on top. Lock lid.
2. Press the Manual or Pressure Cook button and adjust time to 3 minutes. When timer beeps, quick-release pressure until float valve drops. Unlock lid.
3. Transfer to bowls. Serve warm.

Steamed Trout With Garlic & Fresh Herbs

Servings: 2

Cooking Time: 25 Minutes

Ingredients:

- 2 fresh trout pieces
- 1 tbsp fresh mint, chopped
- ¼ tsp fresh thyme, chopped
- 3 garlic cloves, chopped
- 3 tbsp olive oil
- 2 tbsp fresh lemon juice
- 1 tsp sea salt
- 1 tbsp chili

Directions:

1. In a bowl, mix mint, thyme, garlic, olive oil, lemon juice, chili, and salt. Stir to combine. Spread the abdominal cavity of the fish and brush with the marinade. Brush the fish from the outside and set aside. Insert the trivet in Instant Pot. Pour in 1 cup of water and place the trout on top. Seal the lid and cook on Steam for 15 minutes on High Pressure. Do a quick release. Serve.

Mustard Salmon

Servings: 2

Cooking Time: 15 Minutes

Ingredients:

- 2 salmon fillets
- Salt and pepper to taste
- 1 rosemary sprig
- 1 thyme sprig
- 1 tbsp parsley, chopped
- 1 tbsp olive oil
- 2 tsp Dijon mustard

Directions:

1. Pour 1 cup of water into your Instant Pot and fit in a trivet. Brush the salmon fillets with mustard and place it skin-side down on the rack. Top with olive oil, rosemary, thyme, and parsley. Season with salt and pepper. Seal the lid, select Manual, and cook for 5 minutes on High. Once done, perform a quick pressure release. Serve.

Vegan & Vegetarian

Penne Pasta With Shiitake & Vegetables

Servings: 4
Cooking Time: 20 Minutes
Ingredients:

- 6 oz shiitake mushrooms, chopped
- 6 oz penne pasta
- 2 garlic cloves, crushed
- 1 carrot, chopped into strips
- 6 oz zucchini cut into strips
- 6 oz finely chopped leek
- 4 oz baby spinach
- 3 tbsp oil
- 2 tbsp soy sauce
- 1 tbsp ground ginger
- ½ tbsp salt

Directions:

1. Heat oil on Sauté and stir-fry carrot and garlic for 3-4 minutes. Add mushrooms, penne, zucchini, leek, spinach, soy sauce, ginger, and salt and pour in 2 cups of water. Cook on High Pressure for 4 minutes. Quick-release the pressure and serve.

Wheat Berry Salad

Servings:6
Cooking Time: 35 Minutes
Ingredients:

- 3 tablespoons olive oil, divided
- 1 cup wheat berries
- 2¼ cups water, divided
- 2 cups peeled and shredded carrots
- 2 apples, peeled, cored, and diced small
- ½ cup raisins
- 2 tablespoons pure maple syrup
- 2 teaspoons orange zest
- ¼ cup fresh orange juice
- 1 tablespoon balsamic vinegar
- ½ teaspoon salt

Directions:

1. Press Sauté button on Instant Pot. Heat 1 tablespoon oil and add wheat berries. Stir-fry for 4–5 minutes until browned and fragrant. Add 2 cups water. Lock lid.
2. Press the Manual button and adjust time to 30 minutes. When timer beeps, let pressure release naturally for 10 minutes. Quick-release any additional pressure until float valve drops and then unlock lid.
3. Let cool for 10 minutes and drain any additional liquid.
4. Transfer cooled berries to a medium bowl and add remaining ingredients. Refrigerate covered overnight until ready to serve chilled.

Coconut Milk Millet Pudding

Servings: 4
Cooking Time: 25 Minutes
Ingredients:

- 1 cup millet
- 1 cup coconut milk
- 4 dried prunes, chopped
- Maple syrup for serving

Directions:

1. Place the millet, milk, and prunes in your Instant Pot. Stir in 1 cup water. Seal the lid, select Manual, and cook for 10 minutes on High pressure. When ready, allow a natural release for 10 minutes. Drizzle with maple syrup.

Basil Parmesan Sauce

Servings: 4
Cooking Time: 10 Minutes
Ingredients:

- 1 cup fresh basil, torn
- 1 cup cream cheese
- 2 tbsp Parmesan, shredded
- 1 tbsp olive oil
- Salt and pepper to taste
- 2 cups vegetable broth

Directions:

1. In the Instant Pot, stir basil, cream cheese, Parmesan, oil, salt, pepper, and broth. Seal the lid and cook on High Pressure for 5 minutes. Do a quick pressure release and unlock the lid. Serve immediately.

Mushroom & Ricotta Cheese Manicotti

Servings: 4
Cooking Time: 35 Minutes
Ingredients:

- 6 oz button mushrooms, chopped
- 8 oz pack manicotti pasta
- 12 oz spinach, torn
- 3 oz ricotta cheese
- ¼ cup milk
- 3 oz butter
- ¼ tbsp salt
- 1 tbsp sour cream

Directions:

1. Melt butter on Sauté and add mushrooms. Cook until soft, 5 minutes. Add spinach and milk and continue to cook for 6 minutes. Stir in cheese and season with salt. Line a baking dish with parchment paper. Fill manicotti with spinach mixture. Transfer them on the baking sheet. Pour 1 cup water into the Instant Pot and insert a trivet. Lay the baking sheet on the trivet. Seal the lid and cook on High Pressure for 15 minutes. Do a quick release. Top with sour cream and serve.

Quinoa With Brussels Sprouts & Broccoli

Servings: 2
Cooking Time: 25 Minutes
Ingredients:

- 1 cup quinoa, rinsed
- Salt and pepper to taste
- 1 beet, peeled, cubed
- 1 cup broccoli florets
- 1 carrot, chopped
- ½ lb Brussels sprouts
- 2 eggs
- 1 avocado, chopped
- ¼ cup pesto sauce
- Lemon wedges, for serving

Directions:

1. In the pot, mix 2 cups of water, salt, quinoa and pepper. Set trivet over quinoa and set steamer basket on top. To the steamer basket, add eggs, Brussels sprouts, broccoli, beet cubes, carrots, pepper, and salt. Seal the lid and cook for 1 minute on High Pressure. Release pressure naturally for 10 minutes. Remove the steamer basket and trivet from the pot and set the eggs in a bowl of ice water. Peel and halve the eggs. Use a fork to fluff the quinoa. Divide quinoa, broccoli, avocado, carrots, beet, Brussels sprouts, eggs between two bowls, and top with a pesto dollop. Serve with lemon wedges.

Sweet Polenta With Pistachios

Servings: 4
Cooking Time: 20 Minutes
Ingredients:

- ½ cup honey
- 5 cups water
- 1 cup polenta
- ½ cup heavy cream
- ¼ tsp salt
- ¼ cup pistachios, toasted

Directions:

1. Set your Instant Pot to Sauté. Place honey and water and bring to a boil, stirring often. Stir in polenta. Seal the lid, select Manual, and cook for 12 minutes on High.

2. When ready, perform a quick pressure release and unlock the lid. Mix in heavy cream and let sit for 1 minute. Sprinkle with salt to taste. Top with pistachios and serve.

Tofu With Noodles & Peanuts

Servings: 4
Cooking Time: 15 Minutes
Ingredients:

- 1 package tofu, cubed
- 8 oz egg noodles
- 2 bell peppers, chopped
- ¼ cup soy sauce
- ¼ cup orange juice
- 1 tbsp fresh ginger, minced
- 2 tbsp vinegar
- 1 tbsp sesame oil
- 1 tbsp sriracha
- ¼ cup roasted peanuts
- 3 scallions, chopped

Directions:

1. In the Instant Pot, mix tofu, bell peppers, orange juice, sesame oil, ginger, egg noodles, soy sauce, vinegar, and sriracha. Cover with enough water. Seal the lid and cook for 2 minutes on High Pressure. Release the pressure quickly. Divide the meal between 4 plates and top with scallions and peanuts to serve.

Penne Alla Mushroom "bolognese"

Servings:6
Cooking Time: 9 Minutes
Ingredients:

- 1 tablespoon olive oil
- 1 medium yellow onion, peeled and diced
- 3 cups sliced white mushrooms
- 1 jar marinara sauce
- 1 cup chopped fresh basil leaves, divided
- 1 pound penne pasta
- ½ cup vegetable broth

Directions:

1. Press the Sauté button on the Instant Pot and heat oil. Add onion and mushrooms and cook 3–5 minutes until onions are translucent. Add marinara sauce, ½ cup basil leaves, penne, and broth. Press the Cancel button. Lock lid.

2. Press the Manual or Pressure Cook button and adjust time to 4 minutes. When timer beeps, let pressure release naturally for 3 minutes. Quick-release any additional pressure until float valve drops. Unlock lid.

3. Transfer pasta to bowls. Garnish with remaining basil leaves. Serve warm.

Blood Orange And Goat Cheese Wheat Berry Salad

Servings:6

Cooking Time: 35 Minutes

Ingredients:

- 3 tablespoons olive oil, divided
- 1 cup wheat berries
- 2 cups water
- ½ cup dried cranberries
- Juice and zest of ½ medium blood orange
- 1 tablespoon balsamic vinegar
- ½ teaspoon salt
- ¼ cup crumbled goat cheese

Directions:

1. Press Sauté button on Instant Pot and heat 1 tablespoon oil. Add wheat berries. Stir-fry 4–5 minutes until browned and fragrant. Add water. Press the Cancel button. Lock lid.

2. Press the Manual or Pressure Cook button and adjust time to 30 minutes. When timer beeps, let pressure release naturally for 10 minutes. Quick-release any additional pressure until float valve drops. Unlock lid.

3. Let cool 10 minutes and drain any additional liquid.

4. Transfer cooled berries to a medium bowl and add remaining ingredients, including remaining oil. Refrigerate covered. Serve chilled.

Creamy Turnips Stuffed With Cheese

Servings: 4

Cooking Time: 20 Minutes

Ingredients:

- ½ cup chopped roasted red bell pepper
- 4 small turnips
- ¼ cup whipping cream
- ¼ cup sour cream
- 1 tsp Italian seasoning
- 1 ½ cups grated mozzarella
- 4 green onions, chopped
- 1/3 cup grated Parmesan

Directions:

1. Pour 1 cup of water into the pot and insert a trivet. Place the turnips on top. Seal the lid and cook on High for 10 minutes. Do a quick pressure release. Remove the turnips to a cutting board and allow cooling. Cut the turnips in half. Scoop out the pulp into a bowl and mash it with a potato mash. Mix in the whipping and sour cream until smooth. Stir in the roasted bell pepper.

2. Add in Italian seasoning and mozzarella cheese. Fetch out 2 tbsp of green onions and put into the turnips. Fill the turnip skins with the mashed mixture and sprinkle with Parmesan cheese. Arrange on a greased baking dish and place on the trivet. Seal the lid and cook on High pressure for 3 minutes. Do a quick pressure release. Top with the remaining onions to serve.

Plant-based Indian Curry

Servings: 4
Cooking Time: 20 Minutes
Ingredients:

- 1 tsp butter
- 1 onion, chopped
- 2 cloves garlic, minced
- 1 tsp ginger, grated
- 1 tsp ground cumin
- 1 tsp red chili powder
- 1 tsp salt
- ½ tsp ground turmeric
- 1 can chickpeas
- 1 tomato, diced
- 1/3 cup water
- 2 lb collard greens, chopped
- ½ tsp garam masala
- 1 tsp lemon juice

Directions:

1. Melt butter on Sauté. Add in the onion, ginger, cumin, turmeric, red chili powder, garlic, and salt and cook for 30 seconds until crispy. Stir in tomato. Pour in ⅓ cup of water and chickpeas. Seal the lid and cook on High Pressure for 4 minutes. Release the pressure quickly. Press Sauté. Into the chickpea mixture, stir in lemon juice, collard greens, and garam masala until well coated. Cook for 2 to 3 minutes until collard greens wilt on Sauté. Serve over rice or naan.

Easy Cheesy Mac

Servings:4
Cooking Time: 4 Minutes
Ingredients:

- 1 pound elbow macaroni
- ¼ cup unsweetened almond milk
- 1 cup shredded sharp Cheddar cheese
- ½ cup ricotta cheese
- 2 tablespoons unsalted butter
- 1 teaspoon salt
- ½ teaspoon ground black pepper

Directions:

1. Place macaroni in an even layer in the Instant Pot. Pour enough water to come about ¼" over pasta. Lock lid.
2. Press the Manual or Pressure Cook button and adjust time to 4 minutes. When timer beeps, let pressure release naturally for 3 minutes. Quick-release any additional pressure until float valve drops. Unlock lid.
3. Drain any residual water. Add remaining ingredients. Stir in warmed pot until well combined. Serve warm.

Cauliflower Charcuterie

Servings:4
Cooking Time: 2 Minutes
Ingredients:

- ¼ cup hot sauce
- ¼ cup teriyaki sauce
- 1 cup water
- 1 large head cauliflower, chopped into bite-sized florets
- ½ cup ranch dip
- ½ cup blue cheese dip
- 4 medium stalks celery, cut into 1" sections

Directions:

1. Add hot sauce to a medium bowl. Add teriyaki sauce to another medium bowl. Set aside.
2. Add water to the Instant Pot. Add steamer basket to pot and add cauliflower in basket in an even layer. Lock lid.
3. Press the Manual or Pressure Cook button and adjust time to 2 minutes. When timer beeps, quick-release pressure until float valve drops. Unlock lid.
4. Transfer half of cauliflower to bowl with hot sauce and toss. Transfer other half of cauliflower to bowl with teriyaki sauce and toss. Serve warm with dipping sauces and celery.

Coconut Millet Porridge

Servings: 2
Cooking Time: 25 Minutes
Ingredients:
- ½ cup millet
- ½ cup coconut milk
- 2 tbsp coconut flakes
- 1 tbsp honey

Directions:
1. Place millet, milk, and 1/2 cup of water in your Instant Pot. Seal the lid, select Manual, and cook for 10 minutes on High pressure. When over, allow a natural release for 10 minutes and unlock the lid. Drizzle with honey, top with coconut flakes, and serve.

Simple Cheese Spinach Dip

Servings: 6
Cooking Time: 20 Minutes
Ingredients:
- 2 cups cream cheese
- 1 cup baby spinach
- 1 cup mozzarella, grated
- Salt and pepper to taste
- ½ cup scallions
- 1 cup vegetable broth

Directions:
1. Place cream cheese, spinach, mozzarella cheese, salt, pepper, scallions, and broth in a mixing bowl. Stir well and transfer to your Instant Pot. Seal the lid and cook on High Pressure for 5 minutes. Release the steam naturally for 10 minutes. Serve with celery sticks or chips.

Cheddar Cheese Sauce With Broccoli

Servings: 4
Cooking Time: 15 Minutes
Ingredients:
- 1 cup broccoli, chopped
- 1 cup cream cheese
- 1 cup cheddar, shredded
- 3 cups chicken broth
- Salt and pepper to taste
- 2 tsp dried rosemary

Directions:
1. Mix broccoli, cream cheese, cheddar, broth, salt, pepper, and rosemary in a large bowl. Pour the mixture into the Instant Pot. Seal the lid and cook on High Pressure for 8 minutes. Do a quick release. Store for up to 5 days.

Turnip And Carrot Purée

Servings:6

Cooking Time: 10 Minutes

Ingredients:

- 2 tablespoons olive oil, divided
- 3 large turnips, peeled and quartered
- 4 large carrots, peeled and cut into 2" pieces
- 2 cups vegetable broth
- 1 teaspoon salt
- ½ teaspoon ground nutmeg
- 2 tablespoons sour cream

Directions:

1. Press the Sauté button on Instant Pot. Heat 1 tablespoon olive oil. Toss turnips and carrots in oil for 1 minute. Add broth. Lock lid.

2. Press the Manual button and adjust time to 8 minutes. When timer beeps, quick-release pressure until float valve drops and then unlock lid.

3. Drain vegetables and reserve liquid; set liquid aside. Add 2 tablespoons of reserved liquid plus remaining ingredients to vegetables in the Instant Pot. Use an immersion blender to blend until desired smoothness. If too thick, add more liquid 1 tablespoon at a time. Serve warm.

Weekend Burrito Bowls

Servings: 4

Cooking Time: 30 Minutes

Ingredients:

- 2 tbsp olive oil
- 1 onion, chopped
- 2 garlic cloves, minced
- 1 tbsp chili powder
- 2 tbsp ground cumin
- 2 tbsp paprika
- Salt and pepper to taste
- ¼ tbsp cayenne pepper
- 1 cup quinoa, rinsed
- 14.5-oz can diced tomatoes
- 1 can black beans
- 1 ½ cups vegetable stock
- 1 cup frozen corn kernels
- 2 tbsp chopped cilantro
- 2 tbsp cheddar, grated
- 1 avocado, chopped

Directions:

1. Warm oil on Sauté. Add in onion and stir-fry for 3-5 minutes until fragrant. Add garlic and Sauté for 2 more minutes until soft and golden brown. Add in chili powder, paprika, cayenne pepper, salt, cumin, and black pepper and cook for 1 minute until spices are soft. Pour quinoa into onion and spice mixture and stir to coat quinoa thoroughly in spices. Add tomatoes, black beans, vegetable stock, and corn; stir to combine.

2. Seal the lid and cook for 7 minutes on High Pressure. Release the pressure quickly. Open the lid and let sit for 6 minutes until flavors combine. Use a fork to fluff quinoa and season with pepper and salt. Stir in cilantro and divide into plates. Top with cheese and avocado slices and serve.

Traditional Italian Pesto

Servings: 4
Cooking Time: 20 Minutes
Ingredients:
- 3 zucchini, peeled, chopped
- 1 eggplant, peeled, chopped
- 3 red bell peppers, chopped
- ½ cup basil-tomato juice
- ½ tbsp salt
- 2 tbsp olive oil

Directions:
1. Add zucchini, eggplant, bell peppers, basil-tomato juice, salt, and olive oil to the pot and give it a good stir. Pour 1 cup of water. Seal the lid and cook on High Pressure for 15 minutes. Do a quick release. Set aside to cool completely. Serve as a cold salad or a side dish.

Spicy Split Pea Stew

Servings: 4
Cooking Time: 40 Minutes
Ingredients:
- 2 cups split yellow peas
- 1 cup onion, chopped
- 1 carrot, chopped
- 2 potatoes, chopped
- 2 tbsp butter
- 2 garlic cloves, crushed
- 1 tbsp chili pepper
- 4 cups vegetable stock

Directions:
1. Melt butter on Sauté and stir-fry the onion for 3 minutes. Add peas, carrot, potatoes, and garlic and cook for 5-6 minutes until tender. Stir in chili pepper. Pour in the stock and seal the lid. Cook on Meat/Stew for 25 minutes. Do a quick release. Serve.

Vegetarian Chili With Lentils & Quinoa

Servings: 4
Cooking Time: 45 Minutes
Ingredients:
- 28-oz can diced tomatoes
- 1 cups cashew, chopped
- 1 cup onion, chopped
- ½ cup red lentils
- ½ cup red quinoa
- 2 chipotle peppers, minced
- 2 garlic cloves, minced
- 1 tsp chili powder
- 1 tsp salt
- 1 cup carrots, chopped
- 1 can black beans
- ¼ cup parsley, chopped

Directions:
1. In the pot, mix tomatoes, onion, chipotle peppers, chili powder, lentils, cashew, carrot, quinoa, garlic, and salt. Cover with water. Seal the lid, Press Soup/Stew, and cook for 30 minutes on High Pressure. Release the pressure quickly. Add in black beans. Simmer on Sauté until heated through. Top with parsley and serve.

Beans, Rice, & Grains

Coconut Rice Breakfast

Servings: 4
Cooking Time: 25 Minutes
Ingredients:

- 1 cup brown rice
- 1 cup water
- 1 cup coconut milk
- ½ cup coconut chips
- ¼ cup walnuts, chopped
- ¼ cup raisins
- ¼ tsp cinnamon powder
- ½ cup maple syrup

Directions:

1. Place the rice and water in your Instant Pot. Seal the lid, select Manual, and cook for 15 minutes on High. When ready, perform a quick pressure release and unlock the lid. Stir in coconut milk, coconut chips, raisins, cinnamon, and maple syrup. Seal the lid, select Manual, and cook for another 5 minutes on High pressure. When over, perform a quick pressure release. Top with walnuts.

Basic Couscous

Servings:6
Cooking Time: 4 Minutes
Ingredients:

- 2 cups couscous
- 2 ½ cups water
- 1 cup chicken broth
- 1 teaspoon salt
- 1 tablespoon unsalted butter
- 1 teaspoon lemon zest

Directions:

1. Place all ingredients in the Instant Pot. Lock lid.
2. Press the Manual or Pressure Cook button and adjust time to 4 minutes. When timer beeps, let pressure release naturally until float valve drops. Unlock lid.
3. Serve warm.

Spinach-feta Risotto

Servings:4
Cooking Time: 20 Minutes
Ingredients:

- 3 tablespoons olive oil
- 1 small onion, peeled and finely diced
- 2 cloves garlic, minced
- 1½ cups Arborio rice
- 4 cups chicken broth, divided
- 3 tablespoons grated Parmesan cheese
- ½ teaspoon salt
- ¼ teaspoon ground black pepper
- ½ cup julienned spinach
- ¼ cup crumbled feta cheese
- ¼ cup pitted and finely diced kalamata olives

Directions:

1. Press the Sauté button on the Instant Pot and heat the oil. Add the onion and stir-fry for 3–5 minutes until onions are translucent. Add garlic and rice and cook for an additional 1 minute. Add 1 cup broth and stir for 2–3 minutes until it is absorbed by the rice.
2. Add remaining 3 cups broth, Parmesan cheese, salt, and pepper. Lock lid.
3. Press the Manual button and cook for 10 minutes. When timer beeps, let pressure release naturally for 10 minutes. Quick-release any additional pressure until float valve drops and then unlock lid.
4. Stir in spinach and feta cheese. Transfer a to serving dish and garnish with kalamata olives.

Simple Jasmine Rice

Servings:4
Cooking Time: 3 Minutes
Ingredients:

- 2 cups jasmine rice
- 1¼ cups water
- 1 cup chicken broth
- 1 teaspoon sea salt
- 1 tablespoon butter

Directions:

1. Place all ingredients into the Instant Pot.
2. Press the Manual button and manually set the time to 3 minutes. When the timer beeps, unplug the Instant Pot and let the pressure release naturally until float valve drops and then unlock lid. Serve.

Mexican Frijoles Chili

Servings: 4
Cooking Time: 55 Minutes
Ingredients:

- ¼ cup Cotija cheese, crumbled
- 1 tsp olive oil
- 1 onion, chopped
- 3 cloves garlic, minced
- 6 cups vegetable broth
- 1 cup black beans, soaked
- 1 jalapeño pepper, diced
- 1 tsp dried oregano
- 1 tsp dried chili flakes
- Salt to taste
- 2 tbsp cilantro, chopped

Directions:

1. Warm oil on Sauté. Add in garlic and onion and cook for 3 to 4 minutes until fragrant. Add beans, vegetable broth, oregano, chili flakes, salt, and jalapeño pepper. Seal the lid and cook for 35 minutes on High Pressure. Quick-release the pressure. Divide into serving plates. Top with cilantro and Cotija cheese and serve.

Bell Pepper & Pinto Bean Stew

Servings: 6
Cooking Time: 55 Minutes
Ingredients:

- 2 tbsp olive oil
- 1 onion, chopped
- 1 red bell pepper, chopped
- 1 tbsp dried oregano
- 1 tbsp ground cumin
- 1 tsp red pepper flakes
- 3 cups vegetable stock
- 2 cups pinto beans, soaked
- 14 oz can tomatoes, diced
- 1 tbsp white wine vinegar
- ½ cup chives, chopped
- ¼ cup fresh corn kernels

Directions:

1. Set to Sauté your Instant Pot and heat oil. Stir in bell pepper, pepper flakes, oregano, onion, and cumin. Cook for 3 minutes. Mix in pinto beans, stock, and tomatoes. Seal the lid, select Manual, and cook for 30 minutes on High Pressure. Release the pressure naturally for 10 minutes. Add in vinegar. Divide among serving plates and top with corn and fresh chives to serve.

Cheesy Polenta With Sundried Tomatoes

Servings: 4
Cooking Time: 25 Minutes
Ingredients:

- 1 cup sun-dried tomatoes, finely chopped
- 2 tbsp olive oil
- 1 cup onion, diced
- 2 cloves garlic, chopped
- 2 tsp fresh oregano, minced
- 2 tbsp fresh parsley, minced
- 1 tsp kosher salt
- 4 cups vegetable stock
- ¼ cup Parmesan, shredded
- 1 cup polenta

Directions:

1. Warm olive oil in your Instant Pot on Sauté and add in onion and garlic. Cook for 3 minutes until fragrant. Stir in tomatoes, oregano, parsley, salt, and stock. Top with polenta. Seal the lid, select Manual, and cook for 5 minutes on High pressure. When done, allow a natural release for 10 minutes. Top with Parmesan and serve.

Feta & Vegetable Faro

Servings: 4
Cooking Time: 30 Minutes
Ingredients:

- 1 cup faro, rinsed
- 2 cups chicken broth
- 1 celery stalk, chopped
- 4 cups spinach
- 1 bell pepper, chopped
- ½ cup feta, crumbled

Directions:

1. Place faro, broth, celery, spinach, and bell pepper in your Instant Pot. Seal the lid, select Manual, and cook for 10 minutes on High. When ready, allow a natural release for 10 minutes. Top with feta cheese and serve.

Green Goddess Mac 'n' Cheese

Servings: 4
Cooking Time: 20 Minutes
Ingredients:
- 2 cups kale, chopped
- 2 tbsp cilantro, chopped
- 16 oz elbow macaroni
- 3 tbsp unsalted butter
- 4 cups chicken broth
- 3 cups mozzarella, grated
- ½ cup Parmesan, shredded
- ½ cup sour cream

Directions:
1. Mix the macaroni, butter, and chicken broth in your Instant Pot and seal the lid. Select Manual and cook for 4 minutes on High. When ready, perform a quick pressure release and unlock the lid. Stir in Parmesan and mozzarella cheeses, sour cream, kale, and cilantro. Put the lid and let sit for 5 minutes until the kale wilts. Serve.

Harissa Chicken With Fruity Farro

Servings: 4
Cooking Time: 45 Minutes
Ingredients:
- 2 tbsp dried cherries, chopped
- 1 lb chicken breasts, sliced
- 1 tbsp harissa paste
- 1 cup whole-grain farro
- Salt to taste
- 3 tbsp olive oil
- 1 tbsp apple cider vinegar
- 4 green onions, chopped
- 10 mint leaves, chopped

Directions:
1. In a bowl, place chicken, apple cider vinegar, 1 tbsp of olive oil, and harissa paste and combine everything thoroughly. Allow marinating covered for 15 minutes.
2. Heat the remaining olive oil on Sauté and cook green onion for 3 minutes. Stir in farro and salt and pour 2 cups of water. Insert a trivet over the farro and place the chicken on the trivet. Seal the lid, select Manual, and cook for 20 minutes on High. When ready, do a quick pressure release. Open the lid, remove the chicken and the trivet. Add dried cherries and mint to the farro. Stir and transfer to a plate. Top with chic

3. ken and serve.

Hoppin' John

Servings:8
Cooking Time: 35 Minutes
Ingredients:
- 2 tablespoons olive oil, divided
- 1 large sweet onion, peeled and diced
- 1 small jalapeño, seeded and diced
- 2 stalks celery, diced small
- 3 cloves garlic, minced
- 2 cups dried black-eyed peas
- 1 cup basmati rice
- 2 cups chicken broth
- 3 cups water
- 1 ham hock

Directions:
1. Press the Sauté button on the Instant Pot and heat 1 tablespoon olive oil. Add onion, jalapeño, and celery and stir-fry 3–5 minutes until onions are translucent. Add garlic and heat for an additional 1 minute. Add remaining 1 tablespoon olive oil. Add black-eyed peas and toss to combine.
2. Add an even layer of rice. Slowly pour in broth and water. Add ham hock. Lock lid.
3. Press the Manual button and adjust time to 30 minutes. When the timer beeps, let pressure release naturally for 5 minutes. Quick-release any additional pressure until float valve drops and then unlock lid.
4. Dice meat off of the ham hock and discard bone. Stir ham into the rice mixture. Using a slotted spoon, transfer ingredients from the Instant Pot to a bowl and serve warm.

Avocado & Cherry Tomato Jasmine Rice

Servings: 6
Cooking Time: 25 Minutes
Ingredients:
- 2 avocados, chopped
- ½ lb cherry tomatoes, halved
- 2 cups jasmine rice
- 2 tsp olive oil
- ½ tsp salt
- 2 tbsp cilantro, chopped

Directions:
1. Place the rice, 2 cups water, olive oil, and salt in your Instant Pot and stir. Seal the lid, select Manual, and cook for 4 minutes on High pressure. Once done, allow a natural release for 10 minutes and unlock the lid. Using a fork, fluff the rice and add in avocados and cherry tomatoes. Top with cilantro and serve.

Rice & Red Bean Pot

Servings: 4

Cooking Time: 55 Minutes

Ingredients:

- 1 cup red beans, soaked
- 2 tbsp vegetable oil
- ½ cup rice
- ½ tbsp cayenne pepper
- 1 ½ cups vegetable broth
- 1 onion, diced
- 1 garlic clove, minced
- 1 red bell pepper, diced
- 1 stalk celery, diced
- Salt and pepper to taste

Directions:

1. Place beans in your Instant Pot with enough water to cover them by a couple of fingers. Seal the lid and cook for 25 minutes on High Pressure. Release the pressure quickly. Drain the beans and set aside.

2. Rinse and pat dry the inner pot. Add in oil and press Sauté. Add in onion and garlic and sauté for 3 minutes until soft. Add celery and bell pepper and cook for 2 minutes.

3. Add in the rice, reserved beans, vegetable broth. Stir in pepper, cayenne pepper, and salt. Seal the lid and cook for 15 minutes on High Pressure. Release the pressure quickly. Carefully unlock the lid. Serve warm.

Cilantro & Spring Onion Quinoa

Servings: 4

Cooking Time: 15 Minutes

Ingredients:

- 1 cup quinoa
- 2 cups vegetable broth
- Juice of 1 lemon
- ½ tsp salt
- 2 spring onions, sliced
- 2 tbsp cilantro, chopped

Directions:

1. Place the quinoa, broth, and salt in your Instant Pot. Seal the lid, select Manual, and cook for 1 minute on High.

2. Once ready, allow a natural release for 10 minutes and unlock the lid. Using a fork, fluff the quinoa. Sprinkle lemon juice, cilantro, and spring onions and serve.

Cheesy Mushrooms With Garganelli

Servings: 4

Cooking Time: 20 Minutes

Ingredients:

- 8 oz garganelli
- 1 tbsp salt
- 1 large egg
- 8 oz Gruyère, shredded
- 2 cups mushrooms, sliced
- 2 tbsp chopped cilantro
- 3 tbsp sour cream
- 2 tbsp butter
- 3 tbsp cheddar, grated

Directions:

1. Put the garganelli, butter, and salt into the pot and cover with water. Seal lid and cook on High Pressure for 4 minutes. Do a quick pressure release. Melt butter on Sauté and cook mushrooms for 5-6 minutes until tender.

2. In a bowl, whisk egg, Gruyère cheese, and sour cream. Add in garganelli and stir in the mushrooms until the cheese melts. Serve sprinkled with cheddar and cilantro.

Stuffed Mushrooms With Rice & Cheese

Servings: 4

Cooking Time: 25 Minutes

Ingredients:

- 4 portobello mushrooms, stems and gills removed
- 2 tbsp melted butter
- ½ cup brown rice, cooked
- 1 tomato, chopped
- ¼ cup black olives, chopped
- 1 green bell pepper, diced
- ½ cup feta, crumbled
- Salt and pepper to taste
- 2 tbsp cilantro, chopped
- 1 cup vegetable broth

Directions:

1. Brush the mushrooms with butter. Arrange them in a single layer on a greased baking pan. In a bowl, mix the rice, tomato, olives, bell pepper, feta cheese, salt, and black pepper. Spoon the rice mixture into the mushrooms. Pour in the broth.

2. Pour 1 cup of water into the Instant Pot and insert a trivet. Place the baking dish on the trivet. Seal the lid and cook on High Pressure for 10 minutes. Do a quick release. Garnish with fresh cilantro and serve immediately.

Beef Garam Masala With Rice

Servings: 4

Cooking Time: 30 Minutes

Ingredients:

- ¼ cup yogurt
- 2 cloves garlic, smashed
- 1 tbsp olive oil
- 1 lime, juiced
- Salt and pepper to taste
- 2 lb beef stew meat, cubed
- 1 tbsp garam masala
- 1 tbsp fresh ginger, grated
- 1 ½ tbsp smoked paprika
- 1 tsp ground cumin
- ¼ tbsp cayenne pepper
- 3 tbsp butter
- 1 onion, chopped
- 14-oz can puréed tomatoes
- 1 cup beef broth
- 1 cup basmati rice, rinsed
- ½ cup heavy cream
- 2 tbsp cilantro, chopped

Directions:

1. In a bowl, mix garlic, lime juice, olive oil, pepper, salt, and yogurt. Add in the beef and toss to coat. In another bowl, mix paprika, garam masala, cumin, ginger, and cayenne pepper. Melt butter on Sauté and stir-fry the onion for 3 minutes. Sprinkle spice mixture over onion and cook for about 30 seconds. Add in the beef-yogurt mixture. Sauté for 3 to 4 minutes until the meat is slightly cooked. Mix in broth and puréed tomatoes.

2. Set trivet over beef in the Pressure cooker's inner pot. In an oven-proof bowl, mix 2 cups of water and rice. Set the bowl onto the trivet. Seal the lid and cook on High Pressure for 10 minutes. Release pressure quickly. Remove the bowl with rice and trivet. Add pepper, salt, and heavy cream into beef and stir. Use a fork to fluff rice and divide into serving plates; apply a topping of beef. Garnish with cilantro and serve.

Apricot Steel Cut Oats

Servings: 2
Cooking Time: 25 Minutes
Ingredients:

- ¾ cup dry apricots, soaked and chopped
- 1 tbsp butter
- 1 cup steel oats
- A pinch of salt
- 2 tbsp white sugar
- 2 oz cream cheese, softened
- 1 tsp milk
- 1 tsp cinnamon
- ¼ cup brown sugar

Directions:

1. Melt butter in your Instant Pot on Sauté. Stir in oats for 3 minutes. Add in salt and 3 ½ cups water. Seal the lid, select Manual, and cook for 10 minutes on High pressure.

2. When done, allow a natural release for 5 minutes and unlock the lid. Stir in apricots and set aside. In the meantime, combine white sugar with cream cheese and milk in a bowl. In a separate bowl, mix cinnamon and brown sugar. Divide oats between bowls. Top with cinnamon and cream cheese and serve.

Traditional Indian Lentil Soup

Servings: 6
Cooking Time: 30 Minutes
Ingredients:

- 1 tbsp ghee
- 2 tsp cumin seeds
- 1 onion, chopped
- 4 garlic cloves, minced
- 1-inch ginger, minced
- Salt to taste
- 1 tomato, chopped
- 1 cup split yellow lentils
- 2 tbsp garam masala
- ½ tsp ground turmeric
- ½ tsp cayenne pepper
- 1 tbsp cilantro, chopped

Directions:

1. Warm ghee on Sauté. Add cumin seeds and cook for 10 seconds until they begin to pop. Stir in onion and cook for 2-3 minutes until softened. Mix in ginger, salt, and garlic and cook for 1 minute as you stir. Mix in tomato and cook for 3 to 5 minutes until the mixture breaks down. Stir in the turmeric, lentils, garam masala, and cayenne pepper. Cover with water. Seal the lid and cook for 8 minutes on High Pressure. Release the pressure quickly. Serve in bowls sprinkled with fresh cilantro.

Greek-style Navy Beans

Servings: 4
Cooking Time: 45 Minutes
Ingredients:

- 1 cup navy beans, soaked
- 2 spring onions, sliced
- 1 garlic clove, smashed
- 1 tbsp olive oil
- 1 tsp Greek seasoning
- Salt and pepper to taste

Directions:

1. Place beans, 3 cups water, and garlic in your Instant Pot. Seal the lid, select Manual, and cook for 25 minutes on High pressure. Once done, allow a natural release for 10 minutes and unlock the lid. Drain the beans and combine with olive oil, Greek seasoning, salt, and pepper in a bowl. Serve sprinkled with green onions.

Spinach & Kidney Beans

Servings: 4
Cooking Time: 55 Minutes
Ingredients:

- 1 cup kidney beans, soaked
- 2 tomatoes, chopped
- Salt and pepper to taste
- 2 tbsp olive oil
- 1 carrot, diced
- 1 celery stick, chopped
- 1 onion, finely chopped
- 3 cups chicken stock
- 1 cup baby spinach
- 2 tbsp parsley, chopped

Directions:

1. Heat olive oil on Sauté and stir-fry onion, carrot, celery, salt, and black pepper for 3 minutes. Pour in tomatoes, chicken stock, and beans. Seal the lid, select Manual, and cook for 25 minutes on High pressure.

2. Once ready, allow a naturally pressure release for 10 minutes. Stir in baby spinach, press Sauté and cook for 5 minutes until the spinach wilts. Top with parsley.

Spring Risotto

Servings: 6
Cooking Time: 40 Minutes
Ingredients:

- 3 tbsp Pecorino Romano cheese, shredded
- ½ cup green peas
- 1 cup baby spinach
- 2 tbsp olive oil
- 2 spring onions, chopped
- 1 ½ cups arborio rice
- 3 ½ cups chicken stock
- Salt and pepper to taste

Directions:

1. Warm olive oil in your Instant Pot on Sauté. Add spring onions and cook for 3 minutes. Pour in rice and stock. Seal the lid and cook for 15 minutes on Manual.

2. Once done, allow a natural release for 10 minutes and unlock the lid. Adjust the seasoning with salt and pepper. Mix in green peas and spinach and cover with the lid. Let sit for 5 minutes until everything is heated through. Top with Pecorino Romano cheese and serve.

Desserts & Drinks

Stuffed "baked" Apples

Servings:4
Cooking Time: 5 Minutes
Ingredients:

- ½ cup fresh orange juice
- ½ teaspoon orange zest
- ¼ cup packed light brown sugar
- ¼ cup golden raisins
- ¼ cup chopped pecans
- ¼ cup quick-cooking oats
- ½ teaspoon ground cinnamon
- 4 cooking apples
- 4 tablespoons butter, divided
- 1 cup water

Directions:

1. In a small bowl, mix together orange juice, orange zest, brown sugar, raisins, pecans, oats, and cinnamon. Set aside.
2. Rinse and dry the apples. Cut off the top fourth of each apple. Peel the cut portion of the apple. Dice it and then stir into the oat mixture. Hollow out and core the apples by cutting to, but not through, the apple bottoms.
3. Place each apple on a piece of aluminum foil that is large enough to wrap the apple completely. Fill the apple centers with the oat mixture. Top each with 1 tablespoon butter. Wrap the foil around each apple, folding the foil over at the top and then pinching it firmly together.
4. Pour the water into Instant Pot. Set in trivet. Place the apple packets on the rack. Lock lid.
5. Press the Manual button and adjust time to 5 minutes. When timer beeps, let pressure release naturally for 10 minutes. Quick-release any additional pressure until float valve drops and then unlock lid.
6. Carefully unwrap apples and transfer to serving plates.

Cinnamon Applesauce

Servings:8
Cooking Time: 8 Minutes
Ingredients:

- 3 pounds apples (any variety), cored and chopped
- 1 teaspoon ground cinnamon
- ½ teaspoon ground allspice
- ½ cup granulated sugar
- ⅛ teaspoon salt
- ½ cup freshly squeezed orange juice
- ⅓ cup water

Directions:

1. Place all ingredients in the Instant Pot.
2. Press the Manual or Pressure Cook button and adjust time to 8 minutes. When timer beeps, quick-release pressure until float valve drops. Unlock lid.
3. Use an immersion blender to blend ingredients in pot until desired consistency is reached. Serve warm or cold.

Banana & Walnut Oatmeal

Servings: 2
Cooking Time: 20 Minutes
Ingredients:

- 1 banana, chopped
- 1 cup rolled oats
- 1 cup milk
- ¼ teaspoon cinnamon
- 1 tbsp chopped walnuts
- ½ tsp white sugar

Directions:

1. Pour 1 cup of water into your Instant Pot and fit in a steam rack. Place oats, sugar, milk, cinnamon, and ½ of water in a bowl. Divide between small-sized cups. Place on the steam rack. Seal the lid, select Manual, and cook for 5 minutes on High pressure. When done, allow a natural release for 10 minutes and unlock the lid. Top with banana and walnuts and serve.

Peanut Butter Chocolate Cheesecake

Servings:6
Cooking Time: 30 Minutes
Ingredients:

- Crust
- 20 vanilla wafers
- 2 tablespoons creamy peanut butter
- 3 tablespoons melted butter
- Cheesecake Filling
- 12 ounces cream cheese, cubed and room temperature
- 2 tablespoons sour cream, room temperature
- ½ cup sugar
- ¼ cup unsweetened cocoa
- 2 large eggs, room temperature
- 1 teaspoon vanilla extract
- 2 cups water
- ¼ cup mini semisweet chocolate chips
- ¼ cup chopped peanuts
- 2 tablespoons chocolate syrup
- 1 cup whipped cream

Directions:

1. For Crust: Grease a 7" springform pan and set aside.

2. Add vanilla wafers to a food processor and pulse to combine. Add in peanut butter and melted butter. Pulse to blend. Transfer crumb mixture to springform pan and press down along the bottom and about ⅓ of the way up the sides of the pan. Place a square of aluminum foil along the outside bottom of the pan and crimp up around the edges.

3. For Cheesecake Filling: With a hand blender or food processor, cream together cream cheese, sour cream, sugar, and cocoa. Pulse until smooth. Slowly add eggs and vanilla extract. Pulse for another 10 seconds. Scrape the bowl and pulse until batter is smooth. Transfer the batter into springform pan.

4. Pour water into the Instant Pot. Insert the trivet. Set the springform pan on the trivet. Lock lid.

5. Press the Manual button and adjust time to 30 minutes. When timer beeps, quick-release pressure until float valve drops and then unlock lid. Lift pan out of Instant Pot. Garnish immediately with chocolate chips and chopped peanuts. Let cool at room temperature for 10 minutes.

6. The cheesecake will be a little jiggly in the center. Refrigerate for a minimum of 2 hours to allow it to set. Release side pan and serve with drizzled chocolate syrup and whipped cream.

Grandma's Fruit Compote

Servings: 6
Cooking Time: 45 Minutes
Ingredients:

- 7 oz Turkish figs
- 7 oz fresh cherries
- 7 oz plums
- 3 ½ oz raisins
- 3 large apples, chopped
- 3 tbsp cornstarch
- 1 tsp cinnamon, ground
- 1 cup sugar
- 1 lemon, juiced

Directions:

1. Combine figs, cherries, plums, raisins, apples, cornstarch, cinnamon, sugar, and lemon juice in the Instant Pot. Pour in 3 cups water. Seal the lid and cook for 30 minutes on High pressure. Release the pressure naturally for 10 minutes. Store in big jars.

Strawberry Upside-down Cake

Servings:4
Cooking Time: 35 Minutes
Ingredients:

- 2 cups diced strawberries
- 1 cup plus 1 tablespoon all-purpose flour, divided
- ⅓ cup plus 1 tablespoon granulated sugar, divided
- 1 large egg
- 2 tablespoons unsalted butter, melted
- 1 teaspoon vanilla extract
- 1 cup ricotta cheese
- 2 teaspoons baking powder
- 1 teaspoon baking soda
- ⅛ teaspoon salt
- 1 ½ cups water

Directions:

1. Grease a 6" cake pan. Place a circle of parchment paper in the bottom.
2. In a medium bowl, toss strawberries in 1 tablespoon flour and 1 tablespoon sugar. Add strawberries to pan in an even layer.
3. In a medium bowl, beat egg. Whisk in butter, ⅓ cup sugar, and vanilla until smooth. Add remaining ingredients, including remaining flour, except water. Pour batter into pan over strawberry layer.
4. Add water to the Instant Pot and insert steam rack. Lower cake pan onto steam rack. Lock lid.
5. Press the Manual or Pressure Cook button and adjust time to 35 minutes. When timer beeps, quick-release pressure until float valve drops. Unlock lid.
6. Remove cake pan from pot and transfer to a cooling rack to cool for 30 minutes. Flip cake onto a serving platter. Remove parchment paper. Slice and serve.

Spiced Red Wine–poached Pears

Servings:4
Cooking Time: 13 Minutes

Ingredients:

- 4 ripe but still firm pears
- 2 tablespoons fresh lemon juice
- 4 cups dry red wine
- ½ cup freshly squeezed orange juice
- 2 teaspoons grated orange zest
- ¼ cup sugar
- 1 cinnamon stick
- ½ teaspoon ground cloves
- ½ teaspoon ground ginger
- 1 sprig fresh mint

Directions:

1. Rinse and peel the pears leaving the stem. Using a corer or melon baller, remove the cores from underneath without going through the top so you can maintain the stem. Brush the pears inside and out with the lemon juice.

2. Combine the wine, orange juice, orange zest, sugar, cinnamon stick, cloves, and ginger in Instant Pot. Press the Sauté button and then hit the Adjust button to change the temperature to More. Bring to a slow boil in about 3–5 minutes; stir to blend and dissolve the sugar. Carefully place the pears in liquid. Press Adjust button to change temperature to Less and simmer unlidded for 5 additional minutes. Lock lid.

3. Press Manual button and adjust time to 3 minutes. Use the Pressure button to set the pressure to Low. When the timer beeps, quick-release pressure until float valve drops and then unlock lid.

4. Use a slotted spoon to transfer the pears to a serving platter. Garnish with mint sprig.

Amazing Fruity Cheesecake

Servings: 6
Cooking Time: 35 Minutes

Ingredients:

- 1 ½ cups graham cracker crust
- 1 cup raspberries
- 3 cups cream cheese
- 1 tbsp fresh orange juice
- 3 eggs
- ½ stick butter, melted
- ¾ cup sugar
- 1 tsp vanilla paste
- 1 tsp orange zest

Directions:

1. Insert the tray into the pressure cooker, and add 1 cup of water. Grease a springform. Mix in graham cracker crust with sugar and butter in a bowl. Press the mixture to form a crust at the bottom. Blend the raspberries and cream cheese with an electric mixer. Crack in the eggs and keep mixing until well combined. Mix in orange juice, vanilla paste, and orange zest. Pour this mixture into the pan, and cover the pan with aluminum foil. Lay the springform on the tray. Select Pressure Cook and cook for 20 minutes on High. Once the cooking is complete, do a quick pressure release. Refrigerate the cheesecake.

Steamed Bread Pudding

Servings:6
Cooking Time: 20 Minutes
Ingredients:

- 4 cups cubed cinnamon-raisin bread, dried out overnight
- 1 apple, peeled, cored, and diced small
- ¼ cup raisins
- 2 cups whole milk
- 3 large eggs
- ½ teaspoon vanilla extract
- 2 tablespoons pure maple syrup
- ¼ teaspoon ground cinnamon
- Pinch of ground nutmeg
- Pinch of sea salt
- 3 tablespoons butter, cut into 3 pats
- 1½ cups water

Directions:

1. Grease a 7-cup glass dish. Add bread, apple, and raisins. Set aside.
2. In a small bowl, whisk together milk, eggs, vanilla, maple syrup, cinnamon, nutmeg, and salt. Pour over bread in glass dish and place pats of butter on top.
3. Pour water into Instant Pot. Set trivet in pot. Place glass dish on top of trivet. Lock lid.
4. Press the Manual button and adjust time to 20 minutes. When timer beeps, quick-release pressure until float valve drops and then unlock lid.
5. Remove glass bowl from the Instant Pot. Transfer to a rack until cooled. Serve.

Stuffed Apples

Servings:4
Cooking Time: 10 Minutes
Ingredients:

- 4 Granny Smith apples
- 5 tablespoons unsalted butter, softened
- 2 teaspoons ground cinnamon
- ¼ cup packed light brown sugar
- ¼ teaspoon vanilla extract
- ¼ cup chopped walnuts
- ⅛ teaspoon salt
- 2 cups water

Directions:

1. Core apples, leaving some skin on bottom of hole to hold filling in place. Using a paring knife, remove just a little more of the apple center for a bigger area to fill.
2. In a medium bowl, combine butter, cinnamon, brown sugar, vanilla, walnuts, and salt. Stuff apples with this mixture. Place apples in a 7-cup baking dish.
3. Add water to the Instant Pot and insert steam rack. Place baking dish on steam rack.
4. Press the Manual or Pressure Cook button and adjust time to 10 minutes. When timer beeps, quick-release pressure until float valve drops. Unlock lid.
5. Allow apples to cool in pot 20 minutes. Serve warm.

Vanilla Cheesecake With Cranberry Filling

Servings: 8

Cooking Time: 1 Hour + Chilling Time

Ingredients:

- 1 cup coarsely crumbled cookies
- 2 tbsp butter, melted
- 1 cup mascarpone cheese
- ½ cup sugar
- 2 tbsp sour cream
- ½ tsp vanilla extract
- 2 eggs
- 1/3 cup dried cranberries

Directions:

1. Fold a 20-inch piece of aluminum foil in half lengthwise twice and set on the Instant Pot. In a bowl, combine butter and crumbled cookies. Press firmly to the bottom and about 1/3 of the way up the sides of a cake pan. Freeze the crust. In a separate bowl, beat mascarpone cheese and sugar to obtain a smooth consistency. Stir in vanilla and sour cream. Beat one egg and add into the cheese mixture to combine well. Do the same with the second egg.

2. Stir cranberries into the filling. Transfer the filling into the crust. Into the pot, add 1 cup water and set the steam rack. Center the springform pan onto the prepared foil sling. Use the sling to lower the pan onto the rack.

3. Fold foil strips out of the way of the lid. Seal the lid, press Manual, and cook on High Pressure for 40 minutes. Release the pressure quickly. Transfer the cheesecake to a refrigerator for 3 hours. Use a paring knife to run along the edges between the pan and cheesecake to remove the cheesecake and set to the plate.

Peachy Crisp

Servings:4

Cooking Time: 12 Minutes

Ingredients:

- 3 cups peeled, pitted, and diced peaches
- 4 tablespoons unsalted butter, melted
- ½ cup old-fashioned oats
- ⅛ cup all-purpose flour
- ¼ cup chopped almonds
- ⅓ cup granulated sugar
- ¼ teaspoon ground allspice
- ¼ teaspoon salt
- 1 cup water

Directions:

1. Place peaches in a 7-cup glass baking dish.
2. In a food processor, pulse together butter, oats, flour, almonds, sugar, allspice, and salt until butter is well distributed.
3. Preheat oven to broiler at 500°F.
4. Add water to the Instant Pot and insert steam rack. Lower glass baking dish onto steam rack. Lock lid.
5. Press the Manual or Pressure Cook button and adjust time to 8 minutes. When timer beeps, let pressure release naturally until float valve drops. Unlock lid.
6. Place dish under broiler 3–4 minutes until browned.
7. Serve warm or chilled.

Chocolate Chip Cheesecake

Servings:6
Cooking Time: 30 Minutes
Ingredients:

- Crust
- 22 chocolate wafer cookies
- 4 tablespoons unsalted butter, melted
- Cheesecake Filling
- 14 ounces cream cheese, cubed and softened
- ½ cup granulated sugar
- ⅛ teaspoon salt
- 2 large eggs, room temperature
- ½ cup mini semisweet chocolate chips
- 1 cup water

Directions:

1. Grease a 7" springform pan and set aside.
2. Add chocolate wafers to a food processor and pulse to combine. Add in butter. Pulse to blend. Transfer crumb mixture to prepared springform pan and press down along the bottom and about ⅓ of the way up sides of pan. Place a square of aluminum foil along the outside bottom of pan and crimp up around edges.
3. With a hand blender or food processor, cream together cream cheese, sugar, and salt. Pulse until smooth. Slowly add eggs. Pulse another 10 seconds. Scrape bowl and pulse until batter is smooth. Fold in chocolate chips.
4. Pour mixture over crust in springform pan.
5. Add water to the Instant Pot and insert steam rack. Set springform pan on steam rack. Lock lid.
6. Press the Manual or Pressure Cook button and adjust time to 30 minutes. When timer beeps, quick-release pressure until float valve drops. Unlock lid.
7. Lift pan out of pot. Let cool at room temperature 10 minutes. The cheesecake will be a little jiggly in the center. Refrigerate a minimum of 2 hours or up to overnight to allow it to set. Release sides of pan and serve.

Homemade Lemon Cheesecake

Servings: 6
Cooking Time: 1 Hour + Chilling Time
Ingredients:

- Crust:
- 4 oz graham crackers
- 1 tsp ground cinnamon
- 3 tbsp butter, melted
- Filling:
- 1 lb mascarpone cheese, softened
- ¾ cup sugar
- ¼ cup sour cream, at room temperature
- 2 eggs
- 1 tsp vanilla extract
- 1 tsp lemon zest
- 1 tbsp lemon juice
- A pinch of salt
- 1 cup strawberries, halved

Directions:

1. In a food processor, beat cinnamon and graham crackers to attain a texture almost same as sand; mix in melted butter. Press the crumbs into the bottom of a 7-inch springform pan in an even layer. In a stand mixer, beat sugar, mascarpone cheese, and sour cream for 3 minutes to combine well and have a fluffy and smooth mixture. Scrape the bowl's sides and add eggs, lemon zest, salt, lemon juice, and vanilla. Carry on to beat the mixture until you obtain a consistent color and all ingredients are completely combined. Pour filling over crust.
2. Into the inner pot, add 1 cup water and set in a trivet. Place the springform pan on the trivet. Seal the lid, press Cake, and cook for 40 minutes on High. Release the pressure quickly. Remove the cheesecake and let it cool. Garnish with strawberry halves on top. Use a paring knife to run along the edges between the pan and cheesecake to remove it and set it to a plate. Serve.

Homemade Walnut Layer Cake

Servings: 6
Cooking Time: 25 Minutes
Ingredients:

- ½ cup vanilla pudding powder
- 3 standard cake crusts
- ¼ cup granulated sugar
- 4 cups milk
- 10.5 oz chocolate chips
- ¼ cup walnuts, minced

Directions:

1. Combine vanilla powder, sugar, and milk in the inner pot. Cook until the pudding thickens, stirring constantly on Sauté. Remove from the steel pot. Place one crust into a springform pan. Pour half of the pudding and sprinkle with minced walnuts and chocolate chips. Cover with another crust and repeat the process. Finish with the final crust and wrap in foil.
2. Insert the trivet, pour in 1 cup of water, and place springform pan on top. Seal the lid and cook for 10 minutes on High Pressure. Do a quick release. Refrigerate.

Spiced & Warming Mulled Wine

Servings: 6
Cooking Time: 20 Minutes
Ingredients:

- 3 cups red wine
- 2 tangerines, sliced
- ¼ cup honey
- 6 whole cloves
- 6 whole black peppercorns
- 2 cardamom pods
- 8 cinnamon sticks
- 1 tsp fresh ginger, grated
- 1 tsp ground cinnamon

Directions:

1. Add red wine, honey, cardamom, 2 cinnamon sticks, cloves, tangerine slices, ginger, and peppercorns. Seal the lid and cook for 5 minutes on High Pressure. Release pressure naturally for 10 minutes. Using a fine mesh strainer, strain the wine. Discard spices. Divide the warm wine into glasses. Garnish with cinnamon sticks to serve.

Pumpkin Cheesecake

Servings:6
Cooking Time: 30 Minutes
Ingredients:
- Crust
- 20 gingersnaps
- 3 tablespoons melted butter
- Cheesecake Filling
- 1 cup pumpkin purée
- 8 ounces cream cheese, cubed and room temperature
- 2 tablespoons sour cream, room temperature
- ½ cup sugar
- Pinch of salt
- 2 large eggs, room temperature
- ¼ teaspoon ground cinnamon
- ⅛ teaspoon ground nutmeg
- ½ teaspoon vanilla extract
- 2 cups water

Directions:
1. Grease a 7" springform pan and set aside.
2. For Crust: Add gingersnaps to a food processor and pulse to combine. Add in melted butter and pulse to blend. Transfer crumb mixture to springform pan and press down along the bottom and about ⅓ of the way up the sides of the pan. Place a square of aluminum foil along the outside bottom of the pan and crimp up around the edges.
3. For Cheesecake Filling: With a hand blender or food processor, cream together pumpkin, cream cheese, sour cream, sugar, and salt. Pulse until smooth. Slowly add eggs, cinnamon, nutmeg, and vanilla. Pulse for another 10 seconds. Scrape the bowl and pulse until batter is smooth.
4. Transfer the batter into springform pan.
5. Pour water into the Instant Pot. Insert the trivet. Set the springform pan on the trivet. Lock lid.
6. Press the Manual button and adjust time to 30 minutes. When timer beeps, quick-release pressure until float valve drops and then unlock lid. Lift pan out of Instant Pot. Let cool at room temperature for 10 minutes.
7. The cheesecake will be a little jiggly in the center. Refrigerate for a minimum of 2 hours to allow it to set. Release side pan and serve.

Creme Caramel With Whipped Cream

Servings: 4
Cooking Time: 30 Minutes + Cooling Time
Ingredients:
- ½ cup granulated sugar
- 4 tbsp caramel syrup
- 3 eggs
- ½ tsp vanilla extract
- ½ tbsp milk
- 5 oz whipping cream

Directions:
1. Combine milk, whipping cream, and vanilla extract in your Instant Pot. Press Sauté, and cook for 5 minutes, or until small bubbles form. Set aside. Using an electric mixer, whisk the eggs and sugar. Gradually add the cream mixture and whisk until well combined. Divide the caramel syrup between 4 ramekins. Fill with egg mixture and place them on the trivet. Pour in 1 cup water. Seal the lid and cook for 15 minutes on High Pressure. Do a quick release. Remove the ramekins and cool.

Late Night Brownies

Servings:6
Cooking Time: 25 Minutes
Ingredients:

- 2 large eggs, whisked
- 1 teaspoon vanilla extract
- ¼ cup all-purpose flour
- ¼ cup unsweetened cocoa powder
- ⅓ cup granulated sugar
- 2 teaspoons baking powder
- 1 teaspoon baking soda
- ⅛ teaspoon salt
- 4 tablespoons unsalted butter, melted
- 2 tablespoons whole milk
- 1 cup water
- 2 tablespoons confectioners' sugar

Directions:

1. Grease a 6" cake pan.
2. In a large bowl, combine eggs, vanilla, flour, cocoa powder, granulated sugar, baking powder, baking soda, and salt. Stir in butter and milk. Do not overmix. Pour batter into prepared pan.
3. Add water to the Instant Pot and insert steam rack. Place cake pan on top of steam rack. Lock lid.
4. Press the Manual or Pressure Cook button and adjust time to 25 minutes. When timer beeps, let pressure release naturally for 10 minutes. Quick-release any additional pressure until float valve drops. Unlock lid.
5. Remove cake pan from pot and transfer to a cooling rack to cool 10 minutes.
6. Flip brownies onto a serving platter. Let cool completely 30 minutes. Garnish with confectioners' sugar. Slice and serve.

Walnut & Dark Chocolate Brownies

Servings: 6
Cooking Time: 30 Minutes
Ingredients:

- 2 eggs
- 1/3 cup granulated sugar
- ¼ cup olive oil
- 1/3 cup flour
- 1/3 cup cocoa powder
- 1/3 cup dark chocolate chips
- 1/3 cup chopped walnuts
- 1 tbsp milk
- ½ tsp baking powder
- 1 tbsp vanilla extract

Directions:

1. Add 1 cup of water and set a steamer rack into the cooker. Line a parchment paper on the steamer basket. In a bowl, beat eggs and sugar to mix until smooth. Stir in oil, cocoa, milk, baking powder, chocolate chips, flour, walnuts, vanilla, and sea salt. Transfer the batter to the prepared steamer basket. Arrange into an even layer. Seal the lid, press Cake, and cook for 20 minutes on High. Release the pressure quickly. Let cool before cutting into squares. Use powdered sugar to dust and serve.

Hot Cocoa Brownies

Servings:6
Cooking Time: 25 Minutes
Ingredients:

- 2 large eggs, beaten
- ¼ cup all-purpose flour
- 2 packets instant hot cocoa mix
- ⅓ cup granulated sugar
- 2 teaspoons baking powder
- 1 teaspoon baking soda
- ⅛ teaspoon salt
- 4 tablespoons unsalted butter, melted
- ⅓ cup mini marshmallows
- 1 cup water

Directions:

1. Grease a 6" cake pan.
2. In a large bowl, combine eggs, flour, hot cocoa mix, sugar, baking powder, baking soda, and salt. Stir in butter and then fold in mini marshmallows. Do not overmix. Pour batter into prepared cake pan.
3. Add water to the Instant Pot and insert steam rack. Place cake pan on top of steam rack. Lock lid.
4. Press the Manual or Pressure Cook button and adjust time to 25 minutes. When timer beeps, let pressure release naturally for 10 minutes. Quick-release any additional pressure until float valve drops. Unlock lid.
5. Remove cake pan from pot and transfer to a cooling rack to cool 10 minutes.
6. Flip brownies onto a serving platter. Let cool completely 30 minutes. Slice and serve.

Quick Coconut Treat With Pears

Servings: 2
Cooking Time: 15 Minutes
Ingredients:

- ¼ cup flour
- 1 cup coconut milk
- 2 pears, peeled and diced
- ¼ cup shredded coconut

Directions:

1. Combine flour, milk, pears, and shredded coconut in your Pressure cooker. Seal the lid, select Pressure Cook and set the timer to 5 minutes at High pressure. When ready, do a quick pressure release. Divide the mixture between two bowls. Serve.

Appendix : Recipes Index

Chicken Breast Parmesan With Mushrooms 42
Chicken Paprikash 38
Chili & Lemon Chicken Wings 40
Chinese Beef With Bok Choy 31
Chocolate Chip Cheesecake 76
Cilantro & Spring Onion Quinoa 66
Cinnamon Applesauce 70
Coconut Milk Millet Pudding 53
Coconut Millet Porridge 58
Coconut Rice Breakfast 61
Corn & Mackerel Chowder 47
Corn & Sweet Potato Soup With Chicken 41
Creamy Pesto Chicken 35
Creamy Turnips Stuffed With Cheese 56
Creme Caramel With Whipped Cream 78
Crustless Power Quiche 13
Curried Sweet Potato Stew 22
Curried Tofu With Vegetables 17

D

Delicious Turkey Burgers 36

E

Easy Cheesy Mac 57
Easy Chicken Broth 16
Easy Wax Beans With Ground Beef 25

F

Feta & Vegetable Faro 63
Feta Cheese Turkey Balls 40

G

Garlic Lamb With Thyme 29
Georgia Peach French Toast Casserole 8
Grandma's Country Gravy 12
Grandma's Fruit Compote 72
Greek Chicken With Potatoes & Okra 42
Greek-style Navy Beans 68
Green Goddess Mac 'n' Cheese 64
Gruyere Mushroom & Mortadella Cups 32

H

Harissa Chicken With Fruity Farro 64
Herby Crab Legs With Lemon 45
Herby Whole Chicken Stew 17

Penne Pasta With Shiitake & Vegetables 52
Plant-based Indian Curry 57
Pork Chops With Creamy Gravy & Broccoli 24
Pork Loin With Pineapple Sauce 27
Pork With Onions & Cream Sauce 24
Pumpkin Cheesecake 78
Pumpkin Steel Cut Oats With Cinnamon 11

Q

Quick Coconut Treat With Pears 80
Quinoa With Brussels Sprouts & Broccoli 54

R

Rice & Red Bean Pot 66
Ricotta & Potato Breakfast 10
Rosemary Chicken With Asparagus Sauce 38
Rosemary Cod With Cherry Tomatoes 44

S

Sage Turkey & Red Wine Casserole 40
Savory Roast Beef Sandwiches 6
Scrambled Eggs With Cranberries & Mint 21
Seafood Medley With Rosemary Rice 45
Short Ribs With Red Wine & Cheese Sauce 33
Simple Cheese Spinach Dip 58
Simple Jasmine Rice 62
Simple Whole Chicken 37
Smoked Salmon & Egg Muffins 6
Smoky Shredded Pork With White Beans 32
Spiced & Warming Mulled Wine 77
Spiced Mexican Pork 33
Spiced Pork With Garbanzo Beans 28
Spiced Red Wine–poached Pears 73
Spicy Pork Sausage Ragu 30
Spicy Salmon With Oregano & Sea Salt 47
Spicy Split Pea Stew 60
Spinach & Kidney Beans 69
Spinach-feta Risotto 62
Spring Risotto 69
Steamed Bread Pudding 74
Steamed Clams 46
Steamed Leek With Parmesan Topping 20
Steamed Salmon Over Creamy Polenta 44
Steamed Trout With Garlic & Fresh Herbs 51
Stewed Beef With Potatoes 32
Stewed Cod And Peppers 50
Sticky Chicken Wings 39

Strawberry Cream-filled French Toast Casserole 7
Strawberry Jam 9
Strawberry Upside-down Cake 72
Stuffed "baked" Apples 70
Stuffed Apples 74
Stuffed Mushrooms With Rice & Cheese 67
Sweet & Spicy Bbq Chicken 34
Sweet Polenta With Pistachios 54

T

Tangy Shrimp Curry 46
Tasty Chicken Breasts With Bbq Sauce 37
Teriyaki Salmon 44
Thyme Chicken With White Wine 34
Thyme For Lemon-butter Sea Bass 45
Tilapia With Basil Pesto & Rice 50
Tofu With Noodles & Peanuts 55
Traditional Indian Lentil Soup 68
Traditional Italian Pesto 60
Trout In Herb Sauce 49
Tuna & Veggie Egg Mix 47
Turnip And Carrot Purée 59
Tuscan Vegetable Chicken Stew 36

U

Ukrainian-style Borscht 19

V

Vanilla Chai Latte Oatmeal 11
Vanilla Cheesecake With Cranberry Filling 75
Vegetarian Chili With Lentils & Quinoa 60
Vegetarian Soup With White Beans 19

W

Walnut & Dark Chocolate Brownies 79
Walnut & Pumpkin Strudel 8
Warm Shrimp Dip 19
Weekend Burrito Bowls 59
Wheat Berry Salad 52

Made in the USA
Coppell, TX
29 October 2023

23527699R00052